THE SECRET GARDEN

A Play with Music

Based upon the book
by
FRANCES HODGSON BURNETT

Adapted for the stage
by
PAMELA STERLING

Original music
by
CHRIS LIMBER

The Dramatic Publishing Company
Woodstock, Illinois • London, England • Melbourne, Australia

*** NOTICE ***

The amateur and stock acting rights to this work are controlled exclusively by THE DRAMATIC PUBLISHING COMPANY without whose permission in writing no performance of it may be given. Royalty fees are given in our current catalogue and are subject to change without notice. Royalty must be paid every time a play is performed whether or not it is presented for profit and whether or not admission is charged. A play is performed anytime it is acted before an audience. All inquiries concerning amateur and stock rights should be addressed to: THE DRAMATIC PUBLISHING COMPANY, 311 Washington St., Woodstock, Illinois 60098.

COPYRIGHT LAW GIVES THE AUTHOR OR HIS AGENT THE EXCLUSIVE RIGHT TO MAKE COPIES.

This law provides authors with a fair return for their creative efforts. Authors earn their living from the royalties they receive from book sales and from the performance of their work. Conscientious observance of copyright law is not only ethical, it encourages authors to continue their creative work. This work is fully protected by copyright. No alterations, deletions or substitutions may be made in the work without the prior written consent of the publisher. No part of this work may be reproduced or transmitted in any form or by any means, electronic or mechanical, including photocopy, recording, videotape, film, or any information storage and retrieval system, without permission in writing from the publisher. It may not be performed either by professionals or amateurs without payment of royalty. All rights, including but not limited to the professional, motion picture, radio, television, videotape, foreign language, tabloid, recitation, lecturing, publication, and reading are reserved. On all programs this notice should appear: "Produced by special arrangement with THE DRAMATIC PUBLISHING COMPANY of Woodstock, Illinois."

©MCMXCI
Playbook by
PAMELA STERLING
Music by
CHRIS LIMBER
Based on the book by
FRANCES HODGSON BURNETT
Printed in the United States of America
All Rights Reserved
(THE SECRET GARDEN)

Cover design by Susan Carle

ISBN 0-87129-152-5

THE SECRET GARDEN

A Play in Three Acts With Music
For 5 Men and 3 Women and 1 Man or Woman*

CHARACTERS

MARY LENNOX .... 10 years old
MRS. MEDLOCK .... middle-aged housekeeper at Misselthwaite Manor
MARTHA SOWERBY .... 20 years old, housemaid at Misselthwaite
DICKON SOWERBY .... 12 to 16 years old, Martha's brother
ARCHIBALD CRAVEN .... 40-50 years old, the master of Misselthwaite and Mary's guardian
COLIN CRAVEN .... 10 years old, Mary's cousin
BEN WEATHERSTAFF .... 60-70 years old, gardener of Misselthwaite
DOCTOR CRAVEN .... 30-40 years old, Mr. Craven's cousin and Colin's doctor
THE ROBIN* .... a puppet which may be manipulated by an actor costumed in period dress and seen by the audience

TIME: 1911.

PLACE: An unspecified British colony of East India and on the grounds and interior of Misselthwaite Manor in Yorkshire, England.

THE SECRET GARDEN was commissioned by the Muny/Student Theatre Project and produced with the following:

Director	Wayne Salomon
Executive Director	Pamela Sterling
Assistant Director	Christine Murray
Musical Director	Christopher Jackson
Costume Design	Joyce Kogut
Set Design	Kim Conway-Wilson
Lighting Design	Greg Hillmar
Stage Manager	Margaret Terranova

CAST

Mary Lennox	Rachael Weiner
Mrs. Medlock	Jane O'Malley
Martha Sowerby	Mary Warburton
Dickon Sowerby	Bart Shatto
Archibald Craven	John Flack
Colin Craven	Nicholas Weil
Ben Weatherstaff	James Paul
Doctor Craven	Kirk Davis
The Robin	Erin Kelley

MUSICIANS

Piano	Joseph Dryer
Flute	Michael Montague
Cello	Susan Brown

The first presentation of *THE SECRET GARDEN* was by Seattle Children's Theatre, Linda Hartzell, Artistic Director.

MUSIC CUES

ACT I
Page No.

Overture
#1 Mary's Travels 7
#2 Martha's Theme 13
#3 Mary Gets Dressed 16
#4 Mary's Theme 17
#5 Robin Introduces Himself 18
#6 Ben's Theme 20
#7 Robin Teases Mary 21
#8 Scene Change Sc. 3 21
#9 Martha Describes the Garden 23
#10 Sc. 3 Button 25
#11 Sc. 4 Underscore 25
#12 Martha Shows Mary How to Skip 26
#13 Robin Watches Mary 28
#14 Robin Teaches Mary His Song 29
#15 Robin Shows Mary the Key 29
#16 Act I Tag 30

ACT II

Act II Opening 31
#1 Mary Works in the Garden 31
#2 Mary Returns for Dinner 31
#3 Scene Change/Ben Talks to the Robin 34
#4 Dickon's Theme 36
#5 Robin Chirps About Mary 37
#6 Mary Takes Dickon to the Garden 38
#7 Examining the Garden 39
#8 Robin Agrees 40
#9 Scene Tag 40
#10 Mrs. Medlock's Theme 41

#11 Mary's Request 43
#12 Dickon's Letter Into Scene Change 44
#13 Mary Finds Colin 45
#14 Mrs. Craven's Picture 48
#15 Lullaby/Act II Playout (Raja Theme) 49

ACT III
#1 Prelude/Into Opening Underscore 50
#2 Raja/Martha Underscore 55
#3 Garden Theme 59
#4 Dickon Closes the Secret Garden 61
#5 Exit and Underscore 64
#6 Raja Theme 66
#7 Live Forever Underscore 66
#8 Colin Stands Up 69
#9 Planting the Rose 71
#10 Ben's Narration Into Scene 4 72
#11 Quick Changes 73
#12 The Golden Summer 75
#13 Finale: Mr. Craven's Travels 77
#14 Bows

ACT ONE

SCENE: *MUSIC IN [I, #1], an eerie East Indian melody plays as the house lights fade and the stage lights slowly come up. The COMPANY enters, EACH member taking a line of narration in story theatre style. They surround MARY who is by herself center stage.*

NARRATION. When Mary Lennox was sent to Misselthwaite Manor to live with her uncle everybody said she was the most disagreeable looking child ever seen.

It was true, too.

She had a little thin face and a little thin body, thin light hair and a sour expression.

Her hair was yellow, and her face was yellow because she had been born in India and had always been ill in one way or another.

(Lights up on MARY.)

NARRATION. One frightfully hot morning when she was about nine years old Mary awakened feeling very cross, and she became crosser still when she saw that the servant who stood by her bedside was not her Ayah.
MARY. Why did you come? I will not let you stay. Send my Ayah to me.

WOMAN. It is not possible for the Ayah to come to Missy Sahib.

MARY. Send my Ayah to me or I will beat you! *(MUSIC OUT. Sounds of whispering underscore the next lines. FIGURES cross and swirl around MARY but no one speaks directly to her.)* Where is my Ayah? *(More whispers.)* Send my Ayah to me! *(Whispers continue, fading out as COMPANY exits. A MAN and a WOMAN remain.)*

MAN. She wandered out into the garden and began to play by herself under a tree near the veranda.

WOMAN. She pretended she was making a flower bed, and she muttered to herself the names she would call her Ayah when she returned. *(MUSIC IN.)*

MARY. Pig! Pig! Daughter of pigs! *(Lights up on MAN and WOMAN who turn to each other... Lights should not be up full and MAN and WOMAN should be in profile and partly in shadow.)*

WOMAN. Is it so very bad?

MAN. Awfully, Mrs. Lennox. You ought to have gone to the hills two weeks ago.

WOMAN. Oh, I know I ought! I only stayed to go to that silly dinner party. What a fool I was! *(Voices start an eerie wailing. MAN, WOMAN and MARY look up.)* What is it?

MAN. Someone has died. You did not tell me the cholera had broken out among your servants.

WOMAN. I did not know! Come with me. Come with me! *(MAN and WOMAN exit. The wailings grow, underscored by MUSIC. Shadowy FIGURES cross the stage, ignoring MARY who wanders and finally ends in her bedroom, crawling under the covers to shut out the sounds. The wailings and MUSIC eventually die down,*

Act I THE SECRET GARDEN Page 9

leaving an even more eerie quiet. Muffled voices are heard which cause MARY to lift her head. Two FIGURES in white are seen.)

A MAN. Barney! There is a child here! A child alone! In a place like this. Mercy on us, who is she?

MARY. I am Mary Lennox. I fell asleep when everyone had the cholera and I have only just wakened up. Why does nobody come?

BARNEY. It is the child no one ever saw. She has actually been forgotten.

MARY. Why was I forgotten? *(Stamps her foot.)* Why does nobody come?

BARNEY. Poor little kid. There is nobody left to come. *(MUSIC IN as MARY is taken from her bed and given a black cape and hat with a veil during the following narration.)*

NARRATION. It was in that strange and sudden way that Mary found out she had neither father nor mother left; that they had died and been carried away in the night, and that the few native servants who had not died also had left the house as quickly as they could get out of it, none of them even remembering that there was a Missie Sahib. *(MARY is brought forward and COMPANY surrounds her in a semi-circle.)*

A MAN. Mary knew that she was not going to stay at the English clergyman's house where she was taken at first.

A WOMAN. She did not want to stay. *(MARY sits and begins to pantomime playing in the earth as COMPANY chants in rhythm to MUSIC.)*

COMPANY. Mistress Mary, quite contrary,
   How does your garden grow?
   With silver bells and cockle shells
   And marigolds all in a row!

MARY. I don't want boys. Go away!

A BOY. You are going to be sent home at the end of the week. And we're glad of it.

MARY. I'm glad of it, too. *(Pause.)* Where is home?

BOY. She doesn't know where home is! It's England, of course. You are going to your uncle. His name is Archibald Craven.

MARY. I don't know anything about him.

BOY. He lives in a great big old house in the country, called Misselthwaite Manor, and no one goes near him. He's a hunchback and he's horrid!

MARY. I don't believe you!

BOY. It doesn't matter whether you believe me or not. It's true!

MARY. It is not!

BOY. Is! *(MUSIC IN.)*

MARY. Isn't!

BOY *(lines overlapping with MARY's)*. Mistress Mary, quite contrary...

MARY. You stop that.

BOY. How does your garden grow.

MARY. Stop it!

BOY. With silver bells and cockle shells and sour maids all in a row! (He laughs and runs off. *(MUSIC with the sound of a train fading in under as MARY is once more brought forward by MRS. MEDLOCK and another WOMAN.)*

WOMAN. Mary made the long voyage to England under the care of an officer's wife who was glad to hand the child over to the woman Mr. Archibald Craven sent to meet her in London.

MRS. MEDLOCK. The woman was his housekeeper at Misselthwaite Manor, and her name was Mrs. Medlock. *(MUSIC OUT, train sounds continue.)*

Act I   THE SECRET GARDEN   Page 11

WOMAN. Mary sat in her corner of the railway carriage and looked plain and fretful. *(WOMAN exits.)*

MRS. MEDLOCK. I suppose I may as well tell you something about where you are going to. Do you know anything about your uncle?

MARY. No.

MRS. MEDLOCK. Never heard your father and mother talk about him?

MARY. No.

MRS. MEDLOCK. Hmph...I suppose you might as well be told something—to prepare you. You are going to a strange place...*(She looks at MARY who does not respond.)* What do you think of that?

MARY. Nothing. I know nothing of such things.

MRS. MEDLOCK. Eh! But you are like an old woman... Well, it's a grand big place in a gloomy way and Mr. Craven's proud of it in his way—and that's gloomy enough too. *(Her voice begins to fade as MUSIC resumes. She continues to pantomime talking and MARY continues to look out the train window. MUSIC continues under the train sounds which also eventually fade, leaving just MUSIC under the narration.)* The house is six hundred years old and it's on the edge of a moor and there's near a hundred...

(COMPANY enters and set up Misselthwaite during the narration.)

NARRATION. It sounded like something in a book and it did not make Mary feel cheerful.

A house on the edge of a moor—

Whatsoever a moor was...

Sounded dreary.

A man with a crooked back who shut himself up also!

On and on they drove through the darkness. The trees which nearly met overhead made it seem as if they were driving through a long vault.

They drove out of the vault into a clear space and stopped before an immense stone house.

The entrance opened into an enormous hall...

Which was so dimly lighted that the faces in the portraits on the walls...

And the figures in the suits of armor...

Made Mary feel that she did not want to look at them.

Mary Lennox was led up a broad staircase...

And down a long corridor...

And up a short flight of steps and through another corridor...

And another...

Until a door opened in a wall and she found herself in a room with a fire in it and supper on a table.

Act I THE SECRET GARDEN Page 13

MRS. MEDLOCK. Well, here you are! This room and the next are where you'll live—and you must keep to them. Don't you forget that! *(She exits.)*

NARRATION. It was in this way that Mistress Mary arrived at Misselthwaite Manor. *(MUSIC OUT as MARY takes off her cape and hat.)*

And she perhaps had never felt quite so contrary in all her life. *(MARY throws her clothes and herself onto the bed. MUSIC TAG. Lights out. End of Scene.)*

SCENE TWO

SCENE: *MUSIC [I, #2]. The following morning. MARY awakens to find MARTHA, a cheerful young woman, bustling about the room. She is dusting, polishing the grate on the fireplace, humming a snatch of a song. MUSIC fades as MARTHA continues to sing. She turns to MARY and greets her.*

MARTHA. Eh! Tha's awake at last. I'll wager tha' was fair faintin' from thy trip. Tha's slept a good long time but Mrs. Medlock said...

MARY *(interrupts her impatiently).* Who are you?

MARTHA. I'm Martha. Martha Sowerby. An' tha'rt Mistress Mary...

MARY. I know who I am and you will call me *Miss* Mary. *(She points out the window.)* What is that?

MARTHA *(looking out the window).* That's the moor. Does tha' like it?

MARY. No, I hate it.

MARTHA. That's because tha'rt not used to it. Tha' thinks it's too big an' bare now, but tha' will like it.

MARY. Do you?

MARTHA. Aye, that I do. It's fair lovely in spring an' summer when th' gorse an' broom an' heather's in flower. It smells o' honey an' there's such a lot o' fresh air an' th' sky looks so high an' th' bees an' skylarks make such a nice noise hummin' an' singin'. Eh! I wouldn't live away from the moor for anythin'.

MARY. Are you going to be my servant?

MARTHA *(goes back to her work)*. I'm Mrs. Medlock's servant. An' she's Mr. Craven's. I'm to do the housemaid's work up here an' wait on you a bit. But you won't need much waitin' on.

MARY. Who is going to dress me?

MARTHA *(stops a minute to look at MARY in amazement)*. Canna' thy dress thysel'?

MARY. What do you mean? I don't understand your language.

MARTHA. Eh! I forgot. Mrs. Medlock told me I'd have to be careful or you wouldn't understand my Yorkshire. I mean can't you put on your own clothes?

MARY. No. I never did in my life. My Ayah dressed me, of course.

MARTHA. Well, it's time tha' should learn. My mother always said she couldn't see why grand people's children didn't turn out fair fools what with nurses an' bein' washed an' dressed an' bein' took out to walk as if they was puppies.

MARY. It is different in India.

MARTHA. I dare say it's because there's such a lot of heathens there instead o' respectable English people.

When I heard you was comin' from India I thought you was a heathen too.

MARY *(spluttering in anger)*. What! What! You thought I was a native!

MARTHA *(continuing unruffled)*. Aye. An' I was fair disappointed to see tha' was no different from me, for all tha's so yeller.

MARY *(overriding, her anger mounting)*. You—You—Daughter of a pig!

MARTHA *(putting her hands on her hips)*. Who are you callin' names? That's no way for a young lady to talk. Why if you was one of my brothers or sisters I'd give you a good hidin'!

MARY *(losing control and working herself into a tantrum)*. You thought I was a native! You dared! You don't know anything about natives. They are not people—they're servants who must salaam to you. *(Throwing herself on the ground and beating the floor.)* You know nothing about India. You know nothing about anything! *(She sobs uncontrollably.)*

MARTHA *(alarmed)*. Eh! You mustn't cry like that there! I didn't know you'd be vexed. I don't know anythin' about anythin'—just like you said. I beg your pardon, Miss. Do stop cryin'. *(MARY gradually calms down.)* There, that's a good girl. I'll wager tha'll feel better when tha's had thy breakfast. It's time for thee to get up now. I'll help thee on with thy clothes if tha'll get up off the floor. *(She picks up a dress from the chair and holds it up. MARY looks at it with cool approval then sits on the bed and sticks her feet out.)* What is tha' doin'? Canna' tha' put on thy own shoes?

MARY. My Ayah always did it. It was the custom.

MARTHA *(plops the shoes in MARY's lap).* Hasn't tha' got good sense? Our Susan Ann is twice as sharp as thee an' she's only four year old. *(MUSIC IN [I, #3]. MARY is stung by this remark. She grabs the shoes and puts them on, getting them on the wrong feet and struggling with the buttons. MARTHA watches in amusement for a moment and then begins to help her, speaking as she does so.)* Eh! None of my brothers or sisters would ever get dressed if they waited for someone to do it for 'em. Nor eat, neither. You should see 'em all. There's twelve of us an' my father only gets sixteen shillin's a week. I can tell you, my mother's put to it to get porridge for 'em all. They tumble about on th' moor an' play there all day an' Mother says th' air of th' moor fattens 'em. She says she believes they eat th' grass same as th' wild ponies do. *(MUSIC OUT.)* Our Dickon, he's fourteen years old and he's got a pony he calls his own.

MARY. I've never had a pet. There were mostly snakes and elephants in India.

MARTHA. Eh! I'll warrant our Dickon could make friends with 'em. He's a kind lad an' animals likes him. If tha's ready for thy breakfast now, the porridge is still hot.

MARY. I don't want it.

MARTHA *(looking at her, speculatively).* If our children was at this table they'd clean it bare in five minutes.

MARY. Why?

MARTHA. Why? Because they scarce ever had their stomachs full in their lives.

MARY. Why don't you take it to them?

MARTHA *(with a touch of pride).* It's not mine. An' this isn't my day out. I get my day out once a month. Same as the rest. Then I go home an' clean up for Mother an' give her a day's rest.

MARY. I'll have some tea and toast.

MARTHA *(removes the porridge and hands MARY the toast)*. When you're finished you can wrap up warm an' run out an' play. It'll do you good an' give you some stomach for your meat.

MARY. Out? Why should I go out on a day like this?

MARTHA. Well, if tha' doesn't go out, tha'll have to stay in an' what has tha' got to do?

MARY. Who will go with me?

MARTHA. You'll go by yourself. Our Dickon goes off on the moor by himself an' plays for hours. That's how he made friends with th' pony. He's got sheep on th' moors as knows him an' birds as comes an' eats out of his hands.

MARY. I guess I'll go out.

MARTHA. Here's thy hat an' coat. Now, if tha' goes round that way tha'll come to th' gardens. *(She points the way.)* One of th' gardens is locked up. No one has been in it for ten years.

MARY. Why?

MARTHA *(pauses for a split second)*. Mr. Craven had it shut up when his wife died. He won't let no one go inside. It was her garden. He locked th' door an' dug a hole and buried th' key.

MARY. I didn't know he had a wife...*(Sound of a bell offstage.)*

MARTHA. There's Mrs. Medlock's bell. I must run. Tha'll have to button th' front of thy coat thysel'. *(MARTHA grins at MARY.)* I'm certain tha' can do it. *(MUSIC IN [I, #4]. She leaves and MARY struggles to put on her coat. She finishes, rather proud of her ac-*

complishment. MUSIC changes to a slightly melancholy theme as she wanders outside and stands looking about, rather lost. A refrain is heard... "I know something you don't know..." and MARY looks up to see the ROBIN perched on a tree branch. The flute, which is his voice, continues alone, warbling cheerfully. MARY stands still, listening in delight and as ROBIN finishes she almost smiles and steps forward, raising her hand.)

(ROBIN flies away and MARY drops her hand as BEN WEATHERSTAFF enters, carrying gardening tools. He is surprised by her presence but says nothing, touches his cap and begins to work.)

MARY. What is this place?
BEN. One o' th' kitchen gardens.
MARY *(pointing over the wall)*. What is that?
BEN. Another of 'em. There's another on t'other side o' th' wall and there's th' orchard t'other side of that.
MARY. Can I go in them?
BEN. There's no dog to bite thee. But there's nowt to see.
MARY. What about the other garden?
BEN. What garden?
MARY. The one on the farthest side of the wall. There are trees there. I can see them. A bird with a red breast was sitting on one of them and he sang. *(MUSIC IN [I, #5]. BEN stops his work, breaks into an uncharacteristic grin and whistles. ROBIN appears.)*
BEN. Where has tha' been tha' cheeky little beggar? Has tha' begun thy courtin' this early in th' season? Tha'rt too forrard. *(ROBIN chirps... Early bird gets the worm...)*
MARY. Will he always come when you call him?

BEN. Aye, that he will. He come out of th' nest in th' other garden an' when first he flew over th' wall he was too weak to fly back for a few days an' we got friendly. When he went over th' wall again th' rest of th' brood was gone an' he was lonely an' he come back to me.

MARY. What kind of bird is he?

BEN. Doesn't tha' know? He's a robin redbreast an' they're the curiousest birds alive. Watch him peckin' about there an' lookin' round at us now an' ag'in. He's a conceited one. *(BEN whispers.)* He likes to hear folks talk about him. *(ROBIN chirps.)* Aye, I'm talkin' about you. *(Chirp.)* He's always comin' to see what I'm plantin'. He knows all the things Mester Craven never troubles hisself to find out. *(Chirp.)* Aye, you're the head gardener, you are.

MARY. Where did the rest of the brood fly to?

BEN. There's no knowin'. The old ones turn 'em out o' their nest an' make 'em fly an' they're scattered before you know it. This one was a knowin' one an' he knew he was lonely.

MARY. I'm lonely.

BEN. Art tha' th' little wench from India? *(MARY nods.)* Then no wonder tha'rt lonely. Tha'll be lonelier before tha's done. *(He goes back to work.)*

MARY. What's your name?

BEN. Ben Weatherstaff. I'm lonely mysel' except when he's with me. He's th' only friend I've got.

MARY. I have no friends at all. I never had. My Ayah didn't like me and I never played with anyone.

BEN. Tha' an' me are a good bit alike. We're neither of us good lookin' an' we're both of us as sour as we look.

MARY. How dare you...

BEN. Aye, we've got the same nasty tempers, I'll warrant.

MARY. You...you...

BEN. Aye?

MARY. Nothing. *(BEN goes back to work. MARY stands kicking the ground when suddenly ROBIN bursts into a short scrap of song.)* What did he do that for?

BEN. Dang me if he hasn't took a fancy to thee.

MARY. To me? *(ROBIN chirps.)* Would you make friends with me? *(Chirp.)* Would you? *(Chirp, chirp...ROBIN continues softly under dialogue.)*

BEN. Why, tha' said that as nice an' human as if tha' was a real child instead of a sharp old woman. Tha' said it almost like Dickon talks to his wild things on th' moor.

MARY *(turning to him sharply)*. Do you know Dickon?

BEN. Everybody knows him. Dickon's wanderin' about everywhere. Th' very blackberries and heather bells knows him.

MARY. Does Dickon ever come...*(ROBIN finishes his song and flies away.)* He has flown over the wall! *(MUSIC IN [I, #6].)* He has flown into the orchard—he has flown across the other wall—into the garden where there is no door!

BEN. He came out o' th' egg there. If he's courtin' he's makin' up to some young madam of a robin that lives among th' old rose trees there.

MARY. Rose trees? Are there rose trees?

BEN. There was ten year ago.

MARY. I should like to see them. Where is the door? There must be a door somewhere.

BEN. There was ten year ago, but there isn't now.

MARY. There must be.

BEN. None as anyone can find, an' none as is anyone's business. Don't you be a meddlesome wench an' poke your nose where it's no cause to go. Here, I must go on with my work. Get you gone an' play you. *(He leaves. MUSIC OUT.)*

MARY. How can there be no door? There must have been one ten years ago, because Mr. Craven buried the key.

(MUSIC IN [I, #7. ROBIN appears again, chirping mysteriously.)

MARY. You know where the door is. I'm sure of it. *(ROBIN chirps again, a little taunting.)* Show me! *(ROBIN chirps indignantly.)* Will you show me? *(Chirp...that's better.)* Please? *(Even better.)* Where is the door? *(I have to go now.)* No, don't leave...*(ROBIN flies away.)* He's gone. I hope I see him again.

(MUSIC IN [I, #8] for scene change and underscoring MARTHA who delivers the narration as MARY returns to her room.)

MARTHA. At first, each day which passed by for Mary Lennox was exactly like the others. After each breakfast she gazed out of the window across to the huge moor which seemed to spread out on all sides and climb up to the sky, and after she had stared for a while she realized that if she did not go out she would have to stay in and do nothing—and so she went out. And after a few days spent entirely out of doors she wakened one morning knowing what it was to be hungry. *(MUSIC OUT.)*

SCENE THREE

SCENE: *The sound of wind and rain. MARTHA looks at MARY's empty plate with satisfaction.*

MARTHA. Tha' got on well enough with that this mornin', didn't tha'?

MARY. It tastes nice today.

MARTHA. You go on playin' out o' doors every day an' you'll get some flesh on your bones an' you won't be so yeller.

MARY *(wanders to the window).* I can't go out today.

MARTHA. Aye, listen to th' wind wutherin' round th' house.

MARY. It sounds as if a giant were trying to get inside.

MARTHA. You could bare stand up on th' moor if you was out on it today.

MARY. Where is the library? I think I'll go there.

MARTHA. No, tha' mustn't. If Mrs. Medlock found thee wanderin' about th' house she'd be very angry.

MARY. I don't care.

MARTHA. Please, Miss Mary. If tha' doesn't care for thysel', think of me. I could lose my place an' then what would Mother an' the little ones do?

MARY. Oh, very well. But you must stay and talk to me.

MARTHA. I have my work to do.

MARY. Please? Just for a little while? I...I'd like you to.

MARTHA. Well, p'raps Mrs. Medlock won't miss me if I stay with thee a while. *(MARY sits on her bed. MARTHA sits beside her.)*

MARY. Martha, why did Mr. Craven hate the garden?

MARTHA. Art tha' thinkin' about th' garden yet? I knew tha' would. That was just th' same with me when I first heard about it.

MARY. Why did he hate it?

MARTHA. Mind, Mrs. Medlock said it's not to be talked about. That's Mr. Craven's orders. His troubles are none servants' business, he says. But for the garden he wouldn't be like he is. *(MUSIC IN [I, #9].)* It was Mrs. Craven's garden that she had made when first they were married an' she just loved it, an' they used to tend the flowers themselves. Him an' her used to go in an' shut th' door an' stay there hours an' hours. An' she was just a bit of a girl an' there was an old tree branch bent like a seat on it. An' she made roses grow over it an' she used to sit there. But one day when she was sittin' there th' branch broke an' she fell on th' ground an' was hurt so bad that next day she died. Th' doctors thought he'd go out o' his mind an' die too. That's why he hates it. No one's gone in since, an' he won't let anyone talk about it.

MARY. I see. *(MUSIC OUT. The wind wuthers some more. Underneath the sound is heard a faint whimpering.)* Do you hear anyone crying?

MARTHA. It's th' wind. Sometimes it sounds like as if someone was lost on th' moor an' wailin'. It's got all sorts o' sounds.

MARY. But, listen—It's in the house—down one of those long corridors. It sounds like a child.

MARTHA *(stubbornly)*. It's th' wind. An' if it isn't, it's little Betty Butterworth, th' scullery maid. She's had th' toothache all day. There's Mrs. Medlock's bell. I must be goin'.

MARY. Martha...*(MARY tries to stop her but MARTHA is gone. MARY wanders her room, goes to the window and looks out. The wind rises and suddenly a draft blows open her door. The wind dies down and MARY hears a cry again.)* There! It is someone crying! And it isn't a grown-up person. *(She goes to the door.)* I wonder if there really are a hundred rooms in this house. *(She steps outside of the room into the hallway. She wanders through the corridors...pools of lights or panels which turn. She continues to wander. Stops, confused.)* I don't know which way to go. How still everything is. *(The cry is heard once more.)* The crying! It's nearer than it was. And it is crying!

(MARY puts her hand near a panel with a tapestry, pulls back the curtain and discovers a door behind the tapestry. MRS. MEDLOCK appears behind her.)

MRS. MEDLOCK. What are you doing here? What did I tell you?
MARY. I turned round the wrong corner and I heard someone crying.
MRS. MEDLOCK. You didn't hear anything of the sort. You come along back to your own room or I'll box your ears! *(She takes MARY roughly by the arm and hustles her back to her room, the accompanying MUSIC becomes faster and rougher, stopping abruptly with MRS. MEDLOCK's line.)* Now you stay where you're told to stay or you'll find yourself locked up. The master had better get you a governess, same as he said he would. You're one that needs someone to look sharp after you. I've got enough to do. *(She slams the*

door behind her, leaving MARY grinding her teeth in rage.)

MARY. There was someone crying—there was—there was! *(MUSICAL BUTTON to emphasize the end of the scene, [I, #10].)*

SCENE FOUR

SCENE: *MUSIC [I, #11] underscores scene change and narration. Scene Four may be done outside.*

MARTHA. Two days later when Mary looked out her window she could scarce believe her eyes...

MARY. Look at the moor! Martha, come and look!

MARTHA. Aye. Th' storm's over for a bit. It does that at this time o' year. Eh! It was pretty this mornin' when I come across th' moor.

MARY. Did you enjoy your day at home?

MARTHA. That I did. An' Mother was that glad to see me, too. We had all the bakin' an' washin' done early in th' day an' then we made each of the children a dough cake with a bit of brown sugar in it. An' in th' evenin' we sat around th' fire and I told 'em all about you.

MARY. About me?

MARTHA. Aye. They wanted to know all about the Indians an' about th' ship you came in. I couldn't tell 'em enough.

MARY. Did Dickon and your mother like to hear you talk about me?

MARTHA. Why, our Dickon's eyes nearly started out o' his head, they got that round. But Mother, she was put out about your seemin' to be all by yourself like. She said, "Hasn't Mr. Craven got no governess for her, nor no nurse?"

MARY. I don't want a governess.

MARTHA. Mother said to me, she said, "Martha, you just think how'd you feel yourself, wanderin' about a big place like that alone, an' no mother. You do your best to cheer her up." An' I said I would. *(Pause.)*

MARY. You do cheer me up. I like to hear you talk. *(Another pause as MARY and MARTHA look at each other shyly.)*

MARTHA. What does tha' think? I've brought thee a present.

MARY. A present?

MARTHA *(going to her carpetbag and rummaging through).* A man was drivin' across th' moor peddlin' and I was sendin' him away because we had no money to buy anythin', when Mother sees th' skippin' ropes with red an' blue handles. She says to me, "Martha," she says, "tha's brought me tha' wages like a good lass an' I've got four places to put every penny, but I'm just goin' to take tuppence out of it to buy that child a skippin' rope," an' she bought one an' here it is! *(She displays it proudly.)*

MARY. What is it for?

MARTHA. For! Does tha' mean that they've not got skippin' ropes in India for all they've got elephants and tigers an' camels? This is what it's for, just you watch me. *(Skipping MUSIC IN [I, #12] as she expertly displays her prowess, only getting a little out of breath.)* I've skipped as much as five hundred when I was twelve, but I wasn't as fat then as I am now, an' I was in practice.

Act I   THE SECRET GARDEN   Page 27

MARY. Do you think I could ever skip like that?

MARTHA. You just try it. *(She hands MARY the rope and MARY gives it a try, only stumbling a few times.)* A skippin' rope's the sensiblest toy a child can have, that's what Mother says.

MARY. I think I like your mother.

MARTHA. I should think tha' would...Go on now.

MARY *(starts out the door, then stops and turns to MARTHA).* Martha, they were your wages. It was your two pence really...Thank you. *(She holds out her hand. MARTHA shakes it awkwardly.)*

MARTHA. Eh! Tha'rt a queer old womanish thing. If tha'd been our 'Lizabeth Ellen, tha'd have given me a kiss.

MARY *(with a touch of alarm).* Do you want me to kiss you?

MARTHA *(laughs and puts her hands on MARY's shoulders).* Nay, not me. If tha' was different p'raps tha'd want to thysel'. But tha' isn't. Run off an' play with thy rope now. *(As MARTHA watches, MARY begins to skip. MARTHA exits and MARY skips to the garden path.)*

(BEN enters and he and MARY almost collide.)

BEN. Well, upon my word! P'raps tha'rt a young one after all, an' p'raps tha's got child's blood in thy veins instead of sour buttermilk. Tha's skipped red into thy cheeks as sure as my name's Ben Weatherstaff. I wouldn't ha' believed tha' could do it.

MARY. I've never skipped before. I can only go up to twenty.

BEN. Tha' keep on. Tha' shapes well enough for a young'un that's lived with heathen. *(MUSIC [I, #13]. ROBIN appears and chirps curiously.)* Just see how he's watchin' thee.

MARY. Do you think he remembers me?

BEN. He knows every cabbage stump in th' gardens, let alone the people. *(ROBIN chirps in agreement.)* Eh! Tha' curiosity will be the death of thee sometime if tha' doesn't look sharp. *(MARY tries a few skips. ROBIN chirps encouragement as BEN begins to work. He sniffs the air appreciatively.)* Springtime's comin'. Cannot tha' smell it?

MARY *(stops her skipping and also sniffs in imitation of BEN)*. I smell something nice and fresh and damp.

BEN *(reaching down and picking up a bit of earth)*. That's th' good rich earth. It's in a good humor makin' ready to grow things. In th' flower gardens things will be stirrin' down below in the dark. You'll see bits o' green spikes stickin' out o' th' black earth after a bit.

MARY *(also picking up some earth)*. What will they be?

BEN. Crocuses an' snowdrops an' daffydowndillies. Has tha' never seen them?

MARY. No. Everything is hot, and wet, and green after the rains in India. And I think things grow up in a night.

BEN. These won't grow up in a night. Tha'll have to wait for 'em. *(ROBIN chirps in agreement.)*

MARY. Are things stirring down below in the dark in that garden where the robin lives?

BEN *(surly again)*. What garden?

MARY. The one where the old rose trees are. Are all the flowers dead, or do some of them come again in the summer? Are there ever any roses?

Act I THE SECRET GARDEN Page 29

BEN (*nods his head at ROBIN*). Ask him. He's th' only one as knows. No one else has seen inside it for ten year. (*He leaves in a gruff. ROBIN whistles... "What a grouch."*)

MARY (*answers ROBIN*). Yes, I think so, too. (*ROBIN chirps brightly.*) You do remember me! You do! (*Chirp.*) Oh, I like you. You are prettier than anything else in the whole world. (*MUSIC [I, #14]. ROBIN chirps in agreement. MARY tries to whistle as he does. ROBIN corrects her. She tries again, a little closer this time. ROBIN encourages her and adds a phrase. MARY can't get it right, starts to stamp her foot, stops herself, then tries a third time. She gets it right or sings the correct notes and ROBIN congratulates her. MARY laughs and begins to skip.*) I'm going to try and skip all around the garden. (*ROBIN chirps a question.*) Yes, of course you may come. (*MARY skips, ROBIN following, then he flies ahead.*) Not that way—Where are you going—Oh, very well. (*She follows him, skipping up to thirty.*) Maybe next time I can skip up to fifty. (*MUSIC [I, #15] ROBIN chirps a command.*) Well, after all it is my first day! (*Chirp.*) What are you trying to tell me? (*ROBIN chirps impatiently.*) You needn't be vexed, that's no way for a young gentleman to...(*Chirps again. Flies down closer to MARY. She looks down at him and notices something at her feet.*) There's something buried here in the soil. (*ROBIN chirps in excitement.*) Is that what you were...(*"I know something..."*) It's a key! It looks like it's been buried for a long time. (*"...you don't know..."*) Perhaps it's been buried for ten years. Perhaps it is the key to the garden! (*"I know something you don't know."*) Well, if it is the key to the garden, then you ought to show me the door; but I don't believe you know! *(ROBIN chirps a command and flies to the top of the wall, moving along it as MARY follows him. He is chirping all the while, encouraging MARY as she searches.)* Is it here? *(Warm.)* Here? *(Warmer.)* Here? *(Hot, very hot! "I know something..." a gust of wind, a magical trill, MARY pushes aside the ivy boughs and the door is revealed. She tremblingly puts the key in the lock, turns it, opens the door and steps inside the secret garden. MUSIC OUT. In breathless wonder:)* How still it is. How still. *(MUSIC IN [I, #16]. Lights slowly fade.)*

END OF ACT ONE

(or if done in two acts, the next scene may continue without MUSIC [I, #16] and [II, opening])

ACT TWO

SCENE: *MUSIC IN [II, opening]. MARY is discovered in the same place as at the end of Act One. She continues with her line.*

MARY. No wonder it is still. I am the first one who has spoken in here for ten years. *(MUSIC [II, #1]. ROBIN alights on a tree branch and gives a trill.)* Well, perhaps not the *first* one. *(ROBIN chirps approvingly.)* That must be Mrs. Craven's tree! *(ROBIN chirps, a little sadly. MARY examines the tree.)* I wonder if it's all a quite dead garden. I wish it wasn't. *(ROBIN chirps in agreement. MARY moves on. She bends down.)* Yes, there are tiny growing things and they might be crocuses or snowdrops or daffodils. *(She finds a stick and begins to dig.)* It isn't quite a dead garden. Even if the roses are dead, there are other things alive. *(She digs some more, throwing off her coat.)* Now they look as if they could breathe. *(The dinner bell rings. MUSIC fades slowly.)* It's time for dinner already. *(Chirp.)* I shall come back this afternoon. *(She stands and picks up her coat.)* I shall come back. *(MUSIC [II, #2]. ROBIN chirps approvingly as MARY leaves the garden, carefully closing the door behind her and making sure no one is about.)*

(MARY runs to her room where MARTHA is setting out her dinner.)

MARTHA. Eh! Tha' has some roses in thy cheeks. Tha'rt ready for thy dinner, I'll warrant.

MARY. Yes, please, Martha. It all looks so good. *(She begins eating hungrily.)*

MARTHA. Mother will be pleased when I tell her what th' skippin' ropes' done for thee.

MARY. Martha, what are those white roots that look like onions?

MARTHA. They're bulbs. Lots o' spring flowers grow from 'em. Dickon's got a whole lot of 'em planted in our bit of garden at home.

MARY. Does Dickon know all about them?

MARTHA. Our Dickon can make a flower grow out of a brick walk.

MARY. Do bulbs live a long time? Even if no one helped them?

MARTHA. They're things as helps themselves.

MARY. I wish...I wish...I had a little spade.

MARTHA. Whatever does tha' want a spade for? Art tha' goin' to take to diggin'?

MARY. This is such a big lonely place and I have nothing to do. I thought if I had a little spade I could dig somewhere as Ben Weatherstaff does and I might make a little garden if he would give me some seeds. Would a spade cost very much...a little one?

MARTHA. Well, at Thwaite village there's a shop, an' I saw a little garden set there with a spade an' a rake an' a fork all tied together for two shillin's.

MARY *(hurriedly wipes her mouth and goes to her purse)*. I believe I've got more than that in my purse. Mrs. Medlock gave me some money from Mr. Craven.

MARTHA. Did he remember thee that much?

MARY. Mrs. Medlock gives me a shilling every Saturday from him. *(She shakes the purse and the money falls into her hand.)* I didn't know what to spend it on.

MARTHA. My word! That's riches! Now, I've just thought o' somethin'.

MARY. What?

MARTHA. In th' shop at Thwaite they sell packages o' flower seeds for a penny each, and our Dickon he knows which is th' prettiest ones an' how to make 'em grow. He walks over to Thwaite many a day just for th' fun of it. We could write a letter to him an' ask him to go an' buy th' tools an' th' seeds at th' same time.

MARY *(hugs MARTHA unabashedly)*. Oh, you're a good girl! I didn't know you were so nice!

MARTHA *(makes no comment on the hug but it is obvious she is pleased)*. Eh! I'll get thee some pen an' ink an' paper. *(She leaves.)*

MARY *(paces in excitement)*. If I have a spade I can make the earth nice and soft, and if I have seeds I can make the garden come alive. *(From far off there is a faint whimpering cry. MARY looks up and starts toward the door.)*

(MARTHA enters.)

MARY. Martha! I heard the cry again! That's the third time, and there is no wind today.

MARTHA *(agitated)*. Eh! Tha' mustn't go walkin' about the corridors listenin'. Mr. Craven would be that angry there's no knowin' what he'd do.

MARY *(indignantly)*. I wasn't listening. I was just waiting for you and I heard it.

MARTHA. Here's thy pen an' ink. When tha's finished with th' letter I'll put it with th' money in th' envelope an' I'll get the butcher boy to take it in his cart.

MARY. But Martha...

MARTHA. I must run now. *(She exits, leaving MARY to her writing. As she sits and begins to write, MARY shakes her head.)*

MARY. This is the strangest house anyone has ever lived in.

(MUSIC IN [II, #3] as lights fade on MARY and come up on BEN in the garden.)

SCENE TWO

SCENE: *MUSIC OUT. BEN is talking to ROBIN.*

BEN. Aye, there tha'rt. Tha' can put up with me a bit sometimes when tha's got no one better. Tha's been reddin' up thy waistcoat an' polishin' thy feathers this two weeks. I know what tha's up to. Tha's courtin' some bold young madam somewhere, tellin' thy lies to her about bein' the finest cock robin on Missel Moor an' ready to fight all th' rest of 'em! *(With a shake of his feather, ROBIN is gone.)*

(MARY enters and surprises BEN.)

MARY. Hello, Ben Weatherstaff.

BEN *(whirls around, a little embarrassed)*. Now, if tha'rt just like the robin. I never knows when I shall see thee or which side tha'll come from.

MARY. He's friends with me now. *(BEN goes back to work and MARY watches him a minute.)* Have you a garden of your own?

BEN. No. I'm a bachelder and lodge with Martin at the gate.

MARY. If you had one, what would you plant?

BEN. Cabbages an' 'taters an' onions.

MARY. If you had a *flower* garden, what would you plant?

BEN. Bulbs and sweet smellin' things. But mostly roses.

MARY. Do you like roses?

BEN. Well, yes I do. I was learned that by a young lady I was gardener to. She had a lot in a place she was fond of, an' she loved 'em like they was children—or robins. That were as much as ten year ago.

MARY. Where is she now?

BEN. Heaven, 'cording to what parson says.

MARY. What happened to the roses?

BEN. They was left to themselves.

MARY. Do roses quite die when they are left to themselves?

BEN. Well, I'd got to like 'em—an' I liked her—an' she liked 'em. Once or twice a year I'd go and work at 'em a bit. They run wild, but they was in rich soil so some of 'em lived.

MARY. When they have no leaves and look grey and brown and dry, how can you tell whether they are dead or alive?

BEN. Why does tha' care so much about roses an' such, all of a sudden?

MARY. I—I want to play that—that I have a garden of my own. I have nothing—and no one.

BEN. Well, that's true. Tha' hasn't.

MARY. Do you go and see those other roses now?

BEN. Tha'rt the worst wench for askin' questions I've ever come across. Get thee gone and play thee. I've done talkin' for today.

(MUSIC [II, #4]. ROBIN enters as BEN leaves and whistles a comment.)

MARY. Yes, I know. But I think I like him just the same. And I believe he knows everything there is to know about flowers. *(She skips down the path, ROBIN accompanying her. Suddenly, ROBIN's song is answered by another pipe. MARY and ROBIN stop.)*

(A soft, gentle voice comes from behind a tree. It is DICKON.)

DICKON. Don't tha' move. It'd flight 'em. *(MARY stands very still as DICKON slowly stands and comes from behind the tree. He watches the creatures leave and then speaks to MARY.)* I'm Dickon. I know tha'rt Miss Mary.

MARY. You—you came.

DICKON *(grins)*. That I did. I got up slow, because if tha' makes a quick move it startles 'em. A body 'as to move gentle an' speak low when wild things is about.

MARY. Did you get my letter?

DICKON. That's why I come. *(Picks up a parcel from the ground.)* I've got th' garden tools. Eh! They are good 'uns.

MARY *(addresses him stiffly, out of shyness)*. Where are the seeds?

DICKON *(taking an envelope from his pocket).* Th' woman in th' shop threw in a packet o' white poppy an' one o' blue larkspur when I bought th' other seeds. Oh, there's a trowel, too. *(He grins again. MARY relaxes and smiles back. ROBIN is heard and DICKON looks up alertly.)* Where's that robin as is callin' us?

MARY. Is it really calling us?

DICKON. Aye, he's callin' someone he's friends with. There he is in th' bush. Whose is he?

MARY. He's Ben Weatherstaff's, but I think he knows me a little.

DICKON. Aye, he knows thee. He'll tell me all about thee in a minute. *(DICKON whistles a question and ROBIN responds. MUSIC [II, #5].)* Aye, he's a friend o' yours. *(He laughs and MARY smiles in delight.)* Does tha' know how to plant these seeds? *(MARY shakes her head no.)* Then I'll show thee how. Would you like that? *(MARY nods her head yes.)* Where is tha' garden?

MARY. I—I—

DICKON. Tha's got a bit o' garden, hasn't tha'?

MARY. Yes, I mean no, I mean I don't...

DICKON. Wouldn't they give thee a bit? Hasn't tha' got any yet?

MARY. I don't know anything about boys. Could you keep a secret if I told you one? I don't know what I should do if anyone found out. *(Fiercely.)* I believe I should die!

DICKON. If I couldn't keep secrets from th' other lads, about wild things' homes an' such, there'd be naught safe on th' moor. Aye, I can keep a secret.

MARY *(takes a deep breath and begins to speak in a rush).* I've stolen a garden. Nobody wants it, nobody cares for it, nobody goes into it. Perhaps everything is dead in it already. I don't know. *(She begins to pace.)* I don't care. I don't care! Nobody has any right to take it from me when I care about it and they don't. They're letting it die, all shut in by itself! *(She begins to cry.)*

DICKON. Ehhhh!

MARY. I found it myself and I got into it myself. I was only just like the robin and they wouldn't take it from the robin.

DICKON *(gently)*. Where is it?

MARY *(gets control of herself and stands)*. Come with me and I'll show you. *(MUSIC IN [II, #6]. As if she were a wild creature, DICKON slowly stands and follows MARY. She leads him to the secret garden and throws open the door.)* It's this. It's a secret garden, and I'm the only one in the world who wants it to be alive.

DICKON *(looking about him in wonder)*. Eh! It is a strange pretty place. It's like as if a body was in a dream. *(He begins to examine the flowers.)*

MARY. Will there be roses?

DICKON. Shhh. *(MUSIC OUT. He nods his head toward the door to remind her that people might be about.)*

MARY *(whispering as well)*. I forgot...Can you tell if there will be roses? I thought perhaps they were all dead.

DICKON. Eh! No! Not them, not all of 'em.

MARY *(pointing)*. That one? Is that one quite alive?

DICKON. It's as wick as you an' me.

MARY. That means alive, doesn't it?

DICKON. Aye.

MARY. I'm glad it's wick! I want them all to be wick! Let us go round the garden and count how many wick ones there are. *(MUSIC IN [II, #7]. They begin to examine the garden.)*

DICKON. They've run wild. But the strongest ones has fair thrived on it. *(A ROBIN trill.)* See here...A body might think this was dead wood, but I don't believe it is down to the root. *(Another trill as MARY looks. DICKON notices something else.)* Why, who did that there?

MARY. I did it.

DICKON. I thought tha' didn't know nothin' about gardenin'.

MARY. I don't. But they looked as if they had no room to breathe, so I made a place for them.

DICKON. A gardener couldn't have told thee better. They'll grow now like Jack's beanstalk. *(MUSIC begins to fade.)*

MARY. Will you come again and help me work here, Dickon?

DICKON. I'll come every day if tha' wants me to, rain or shine. *(Pausing and scratching his head. MUSIC OUT.)* Seems as if there'd been some prunin' done here an' there, later than ten year ago.

MARY. But the door was locked and the key was buried. No one could get in.

DICKON. Aye, that's true. *(He shrugs and goes back to work.)*

MARY *(pauses and looks at DICKON)*. Dickon, I like you, and you make the fifth person. I never thought I should like five people.

DICKON. Only five folk as tha' likes? Who is the other four?

MARY. Your mother and Martha and the robin and Ben Weatherstaff.

DICKON (*lets out a hearty laugh and stifles it with his sleeve*). I know tha' thinks I'm a strange lad, but I think tha'rt the strangest little lass I ever saw.

MARY (*very serious*). Does tha' like me?

DICKON. Eh! That I does. I likes thee wonderful. (*MUSIC [II, #8]. ROBIN chirps.*) An' so does th' robin I do believe! (*Chirp.*)

MARY. That's two then! (*Chirp.*) That's two for me. (*Chirp. She goes back to work. DICKON watches her in amusement. The dinner bell rings and MARY looks up in disappointment.*) I have to go...

DICKON. Run along and eat thy victuals. I'll eat my dinner here an' stay an' work a bit.

MARY (*stands and takes a step. Turns back*). Whatever happens, you—you would never tell?

DICKON. If tha' was a missel thrush an' showed me where thy nest was, does tha' think I'd tell anyone? Not me. Tha'rt as safe as a missel thrush. (*MUSIC IN [II, #9]. DICKON goes back to work. MARY watches him a moment, then leaves as the lights fade.*)

SCENE THREE

SCENE: *Lights come up on MARTHA in MARY's room as MARY enters at a run.*

MARTHA. Tha's late. Where has tha' been?

MARY. I've seen Dickon!

MARTHA. I knew he'd come. How does tha' like him?

MARY. I think—I think he's beautiful!

MARTHA. Well, he's th' best lad as ever was born, but us never thought he was handsome.

Act II   THE SECRET GARDEN   Page 41

MARY. He's going to show me how to plant the seeds, Martha.

MARTHA. Who did tha' ask about a place for thy flowers?

MARY. I—I haven't asked anyone yet.

MARTHA. If I was you, I'd ask Ben Weatherstaff. P'raps he'd find you a corner somewhere out o' th' way. *(MRS. MEDLOCK calls for MARY offstage.)* I clean forgot to tell you. Mr. Craven came back this mornin' an' I think he wants to see you.

MARY. Oh! Why? He didn't want to see me when I came. Mrs. Medlock said he didn't. *(MRS. MEDLOCK calls again. MARTHA continues in a hurried whisper.)*

MARTHA. Well, Mrs. Medlock says it's because o' Mother. She was walkin' to Thwaite village an' she met him. I don't know what she said to him but it put him in th' mind to see you before he goes away again, tomorrow.

(MRS. MEDLOCK enters in a self-important bustle.)

MRS. MEDLOCK. Your hair's rough. *(MUSIC IN [II, #10.)* Go and brush it. And Martha, help her put on her best pinafore. Mr. Craven sent me to bring her to him in his study.

MARY *(as MARTHA helps her to get dressed)*. What does Mr. Craven want to see me about, did he say?

MRS. MEDLOCK. It's not for the likes of you or me to question Mr. Craven's wishes. Now come along, he doesn't like to be kept waiting. *(MUSIC continues as she hurries MARY along the corridor.)*

(Lights come up on MR. CRAVEN sitting in an armchair, reading a book. He looks up as they enter.)

MRS. MEDLOCK. This is Miss Mary, sir. *(MUSIC OUT.)*

MR. CRAVEN. You can go and leave her here. I will ring for you when I want you to take her away. *(MRS. MEDLOCK leaves.)* Come here. *(MARY takes a tentative step forward. They stare at each other a moment.)* Are you well?

MARY. Yes.

MR. CRAVEN. Do they take good care of you?

MARY. Yes.

MR. CRAVEN. You are very thin.

MARY *(stiffly)*. I am getting fatter.

MR. CRAVEN. I forgot you. I intended to send you a governess or a nurse, but I forgot.

MARY. Please...Please...*(She chokes.)*

MR. CRAVEN. What do you want to say?

MARY. I—I am too big for a nurse. And please—please don't make me have a governess yet.

MR. CRAVEN. That was what the Sowerby woman said.

MARY. Martha's mother?

MR. CRAVEN. Yes, I believe so.

MARY. She knows about children, sir. She has twelve. She knows.

MR. CRAVEN. What do you want to do?

MARY. I want to play out of doors.

MR. CRAVEN. Mrs. Sowerby said it would do you good. Where do you play?

MARY. Everywhere. I skip and run about and I look to see if things are beginning to stick up out of the earth. I don't do any harm.

MR. CRAVEN. Don't look so frightened. You could not do any harm, a child like you! You may do what you like.

MARY. May I?

MR. CRAVEN. Please don't look so frightened. Of course you may. I am your guardian, though I am a poor one for any child. I cannot give you time or attention. I am too ill and wretched and distracted, but I wish you to be happy and comfortable. I sent for you today because Susan Sowerby said her daughter Martha had talked about you. I thought her rather bold to stop me on the moor but she said—Mrs. Craven had been kind to her...Is there anything you want? Toys, books, dolls?

MARY. Might I...might I have a bit of earth? *(MUSIC IN [II, #11].)*

MR. CRAVEN. Earth! What do you mean?

MARY. To plant seeds in—to make things grow—to make them come alive.

MR. CRAVEN. Do you care about gardens so much?

MARY. I didn't know about them in India. I was always ill and tired and it was too hot. But here it is different.

MR. CRAVEN. A bit of earth...You remind me of someone else who loved the earth and things that grow. When you see a bit of earth you want, take it child, and make it come alive. *(MUSIC fades.)*

MARY. May I take it from anywhere? If it's not wanted?

MR. CRAVEN. Anywhere. *(He rings the bell.)* There! You must go now. I am tired.

(MRS. MEDLOCK enters. MR. CRAVEN speaks to MARY.)

MR. CRAVEN. Goodbye, I shall be away all summer.

MRS. MEDLOCK. Sir?

MR. CRAVEN. Mrs. Medlock, now I have seen the child I understand what Mrs. Sowerby meant. She must be less delicate before she begins lessons. Give her simple, healthy food. Don't look after her too much. She needs liberty and fresh air and romping about.

MRS. MEDLOCK. Thank you, sir. I'd always take Susan Sowerby's advice about children myself. She's what you might call healthy-minded, if you understand me.

MR. CRAVEN. I understand. Take Miss Mary away now and send my manservant to me. *(MRS. MEDLOCK and MARY leave. Lights out on MR. CRAVEN.)*

MRS. MEDLOCK. Well, I'm glad he's listened to Susan's advice. Susan Sowerby an' me went to school together an' she's a sensible soul...Here you are. Mind now, just because Mr. Craven said you were to be allowed to roam out of doors, you're not to go poking about the house. *(MARY and MARTHA watch MRS. MEDLOCK leave. MARY turns to MARTHA, joyously.)*

MARY. I can have my garden! I may have it where I like! I am not going to have a governess for a long time. I may do what I like— anywhere!

MARTHA. Eh! That was nice of him, wasn't it?

MARY *(getting ready for bed).* Martha, he is really a nice man, only his face is so miserable and his forehead is all drawn together.

MARTHA. I've heard tell he was different when his Missus was alive. People say she married him for his money, but I don't think she did.

MARY. I don't think so either.

MARTHA. Oh! I've somethin' for thee from Dickon. *(MUSIC IN [II, #12].)* He had to go but he said to give this to thee. *(She hands MARY a piece of paper.)*

Act II   THE SECRET GARDEN   Page 45

MARY. But he said he'd stay in the...What is it?

MARTHA *(looking over her shoulder).* Eh! I never knew our Dickon was as clever as that. That there's a picture of a missel thrush on her nest, as large as life an' twice as natural.

MARY. A missel thrush?...Oh...

MARTHA. An' there's some words there, too. What does it say?

MARY. I will *(Spelling it out.)* c-u-m b-a-k...I will come back! *(Lights fade as MARY looks at MARTHA happily. MUSIC continues into scene change.)*

SCENE FOUR

SCENE: *Lights come up with wind and rain sounds as MARY is discovered tossing and turning in her bed.*

MARY *(sitting up and punching her pillow).* The wind is as contrary as ever I was. It came because I did not want it. *(The wind dies down and the sound of heartbroken sobbing is heard.)* It isn't the wind now. It is different. *(More sobbing.)* I am going to find out what it is. *(MUSIC IN [II, #13]. She puts on her wrapper.)* I don't care about Mrs. Medlock. I don't care! *(MARY gets out of bed. She goes to her door and carefully opens it. The crying continues, getting louder as MARY wanders through the corridors of the house. Music plays as she comes to the panel with the tapestry. She pushes back the tapestry, opens the door and enters a bedroom. A young BOY is discovered crying in his bed. He looks up at her with large eyes and speaks.)*

COLIN. Who are you? Are you a ghost?

MARY. No. Are you one?

COLIN. No. I am Colin.

MARY. Who is Colin?

COLIN. I am Colin Craven. Who are you?

MARY. I am Mary Lennox. I heard someone crying and I wanted to find out who it was. Mr. Craven is my uncle.

COLIN. He is my father.

MARY. Your father! No one ever told me he had a boy.

COLIN. You are real, aren't you? I have such real dreams very often. You might be one of them. *(MARY goes to COLIN and pinches him.)* Ouch!

MARY. You see, I am real. Did no one tell you I had come here to live?

COLIN. They daren't.

MARY. Why?

COLIN. Because I hate for people to look at me.

MARY. Why?

COLIN. Because I am like this, always ill and always having to lie down. If I live I may be a hunchback. My father hates to think I may be like him. He hates to see me.

MARY. Why?

COLIN. My mother died when I was born and it makes him wretched to look at me.

MARY *(to herself)*. He hates the garden because she died.

COLIN. What garden?

MARY. Oh—just a garden she used to like...If you don't like people to see you, do you want me to go away?

COLIN *(giving a tug on her wrapper)*. No. I should be sure you were a dream if you went. Sit there. *(He pats his bed.)* I want to hear about you. How old are you?

MARY. I am ten. And so are you.

COLIN. How do you know that?

MARY. Because when you were born the garden door was locked and the key was buried. And it's been locked for ten years.

COLIN. What garden door was locked?

MARY. The...garden Mr. Craven hates.

COLIN. Who locked it?

MARY. He did.

COLIN. Where is the key?

MARY. No one knows.

COLIN. Why?

MARY. No one will talk about it.

COLIN. Why?

MARY. I think...I think they have been told not to answer questions.

COLIN. I would make them. *(There is a pause as MARY digests this information.)*

MARY. Could you?

COLIN. Everyone is obliged to please me. If I were to live, this place would sometime belong to me. I would make them tell me.

MARY *(trying to change the subject)*. Do you think you won't live?

COLIN. Ever since I can remember anything, I have heard people say I shan't. At first they thought I was too little to understand and now they think I don't hear. But I do. My doctor is my father's cousin. He is quite poor and if I die he will have all Misselthwaite when my father is dead. I should think he wouldn't want me to live.

MARY. Do you want to live?

COLIN. No. But I don't want to die either. Let us talk about something else. Talk about that garden. Don't you want to see it?

MARY. Yes.

COLIN. I do. I don't think I ever really wanted to see anything before. They have to please me. I will make them take me there and I will let you go too.

MARY. Oh don't—don't—don't—don't do that!

COLIN. Why? You said you wanted to see it.

MARY. I do, but if you make them open the door and take you in like that, it will never be a secret again.

COLIN. A secret? What do you mean? Tell me.

MARY. You see—if no one knows but ourselves—if there was a door—hidden somewhere—and we could find it—and dig in the garden and play and bring it back to life so the pale green points push up through the green earth because the spring is coming—if the garden was a secret and we could get into it we could see how many roses were alive—Oh, don't you see how much nicer it would be if it was a secret?

COLIN. I never had a secret, except that one about not living to grow up. I like this kind better...I am going to let you look at something...Do you see that curtain?

MARY. Yes.

COLIN. There is a chord hanging from it. Go and pull it. *(MUSIC [II, #14]. MARY pulls the cord and the curtain pulls back to reveal a picture of a lovely young woman. The "garden theme" plays softly.)* That is my mother. I don't see why she died. Sometimes I hate her for doing it. Draw the curtain again. *(MARY does so and the MUSIC fades out.)* I don't like to see her looking at me.

MARY. Why?

COLIN. She smiles too much when I am ill and miserable. Besides, she's a kind of secret—and I think you shall be a secret, too...Do you know Martha?

MARY. Yes.

Act II THE SECRET GARDEN

COLIN. She is the one who is asleep in the other room. Martha shall tell you when I want you to come here.

MARY. Martha knew about you all the time?

COLIN. Yes, she often attends to me.

MARY. Shall I go away now? Your eyes look sleepy.

COLIN. I wish I could go to sleep before you leave me.

MARY. Shut your eyes and I will do what my Ayah used to do in India. I will pat your hand and stroke it and sing something quite low.

COLIN. I should like that, perhaps. *(MARY begins to sing. MUSIC [II, #15].)*

MARY. KHUM PADA NE MASHE PESHE
   KHUM MERE BAH DYIJO
   BATA BHORE PAN DEBO;
   GALE BORE KHEO.

COLIN *(dreamily)*. That is nice. *(MARY continues to sing as COLIN falls asleep, and tiptoes out of his room.)*

MARY. EHSHO MASHI EHSHO PISHI
   KHOCARE KHATE EHSHO
   KHATANE; PALONG ENAI,
   CHOKA PATE BOSHO...

(Lights fade and ACT II Playout, "Raja Theme" plays.)

END OF ACT TWO
(...or ACT ONE)

ACT THREE (or Two)

SCENE: *PRELUDE MUSIC begins [III, #1] and segues to a solo piano playing "Mary's Theme." Lights up on MARTHA and MARY in tableau. MARTHA has some knitting in her hand.*

MARTHA. The moor was hidden in mist when the morning came. There could be no going out of doors. Martha was so busy that Mary had no opportunity of talking to her, but in the afternoon she asked her to come and sit with her. *(MUSIC fades as MARTHA sits and begins knitting. MARY paces.)* Tha' looks as if tha' had somethin' to say.

MARY *(stops her pacing and confronts MARTHA)*. I have found out what the crying was.

MARTHA. Tha' hasn't!

MARY. It was Colin. I found him.

MARTHA. Eh! Miss Mary! If Mrs. Medlock finds out she'll think I broke orders and told thee. I shall lose my place and then what'll Mother do! *(A bell rings.)* That's him ringin' now. I hope he's in a good temper. *(She leaves.)*

MARY *(paces)*. I think he sounds like a very spoiled boy, even if he has been ill a good bit. Well, if he ever gets angry at me, I'll never go and see him again.

(MARTHA returns.)

MARTHA. Well, tha' has bewitched him. "I want Mary Lennox to come and talk to me, and remember you're not to tell anyone," he said. You'd better go as quick as you can. *(MARTHA accompanies MARY to COLIN's room.)*

(Lights up on COLIN who is sitting in bed, a large book in his hands.)

COLIN. Come in. I've been thinking about you all morning.

MARY. I've been thinking about you, too. You don't know how frightened Martha is.

MARTHA. Please, Miss...

COLIN *(interrupting her)*. Martha, have you to do what I please or have you not?

MARTHA. I have to do what you please, sir.

COLIN. Has Medlock to do what I please?

MARTHA. Everybody has, sir.

COLIN. Well, then, if I order you to bring Miss Mary to me, how can Medlock send you away if she finds out?

MARTHA. Please don't let her, sir.

COLIN. I'll send her away if she dares to say a word about such a thing.

MARTHA. Thank you, sir. I want to do my duty, sir.

COLIN. What I want is your duty. I'll take care of you. Now go away. *(MARTHA bobs a curtsey and leaves. COLIN turns to MARY who is staring at him.)* Why are you looking at me like that? What are you thinking about?

MARY. I am thinking about two things.

COLIN. Sit down and tell me.

MARY. This is the first one. Once when I was in India I saw a boy who was a Rajah. He had rubies and emeralds and diamonds stuck all over him. He spoke to his people just as you spoke to Martha.

COLIN. I shall make you tell me about Rajahs presently, but first tell me what the second thing was.

MARY. I was thinking how different you are from Dickon.

COLIN. Who is Dickon? What a funny name!

MARY. He is Martha's brother. He is not like anyone else in the world. He can charm foxes and squirrels and birds just as the natives in India charm snakes.

COLIN. Tell me some more about him.

MARY. He knows about everything that grows on the moor.

COLIN. How can he like the moor when it's such a big, bare, ugly place?

MARY. When Dickon talks about it, it's beautiful.

COLIN. I couldn't go on the moor.

MARY. Why?

COLIN. It's cold, and the flowers make me sneeze. And the gardeners are always looking at me. I hate for people to look at me.

MARY. Why?

COLIN. Because I know they are looking for my hunchback lump. And people are always patting my cheeks and saying, "Poor thing." Once when a lady did that to me I screamed and bit her hand. She looked quite frightened and ran away.

MARY. She thought you had gone mad, like a dog.

COLIN. I don't care what she thought.

MARY. Would you hate it—if a boy looked at you?

COLIN. There's one boy...there's one boy I believe I shouldn't mind. It's that boy you were talking about—Dickon.

Act III THE SECRET GARDEN Page 53

MARY. I'm sure you wouldn't mind him.

COLIN. The animals don't and perhaps that is why I shouldn't. He's a sort of animal charmer and I am a boy animal.

MARY. You are! *(COLIN barks a little and MARY laughs. She barks back and he laughs. And they start to laugh together. COLIN pauses a moment and looks at MARY.)*

COLIN. I just thought of something.

MARY. What?

COLIN. You and I—are cousins!

MARY. We are!

COLIN. And we never thought of it before...

MARY. ...talking all this time...

COLIN. ...last night...

MARY. ...and this morning...

COLIN. ...and we never realized we were cousins!

MARY. Oh, that's funny!

COLIN. It's not that funny!

MARY. Yes, it is!

COLIN. You're right. It is! *(They giggle hysterically.)*

(DR. CRAVEN and MRS. MEDLOCK enter in a hurry and stop abruptly, amazed at the sight of MARY and COLIN laughing so hard they are almost crying.)

MRS. MEDLOCK. Good Lord!

DR. CRAVEN. What is this? What does this mean?

COLIN *(wiping the tears of laughter from his eyes).* This is Mary Lennox. She is my c...c...cousin! *(He bursts into more laughter.)*

DR. CRAVEN *(threatening).* Mrs. Medlock...

MRS. MEDLOCK. Oh, sir, I don't know how it's happened. There's not a servant on the place that'd dare to talk. They all have their orders.

COLIN *(gaining control, once more the Rajah).* Nobody told her anything. She heard me crying and found me herself. I am glad she came. Don't be silly, Medlock.

DR. CRAVEN *(rubbing his hands together in a nervous gesture).* Well, well, well...Hello, Mary. I am Doctor Craven.

MARY. I know.

DR. CRAVEN *(sitting by COLIN and taking his pulse).* I am afraid Miss Mary's visit has excited you, my boy. Excitement is not good for you, you know.

COLIN. I should be excited if she kept away. I am better. She makes me better.

MRS. MEDLOCK. He does look rather better, sir. *(DR. CRAVEN raises an eyebrow. MRS. MEDLOCK amends her statement.)* But, he looked better this morning before she came into the room.

COLIN. She came into the room last night. She stayed with me a long time. I was better when I wakened up. I want my breakfast. Tell them, Medlock.

MRS. MEDLOCK. Yes sir. *(She exits.)*

DR. CRAVEN. Well, my boy, you do seem to be a little bit better, but you must not forget how very ill you are. You must not talk too much, you must not forget that you are easily tired and you must not forget that...

COLIN *(interrupting).* I want to forget. Mary makes me forget. That is why I want her to come and talk to me.

DR. CRAVEN. Very well, Master Colin, if that is what you wish.

COLIN. It is. And there is something else I wish.

DR. CRAVEN. What is that?

Act III   THE SECRET GARDEN   Page 55

COLIN. I wish you would go away and leave me alone with my cousin. *(DR. CRAVEN stands and sighs. He goes out the door, shaking his head. COLIN turns to MARY.)* Now, Mary Lennox, sit here. I want you to tell me more about Dickon and the moor but first, I want you to tell me about Rajahs. *(MUSIC IN [III, #2].)*

(Lights fade on COLIN and MARY and come up on MARTHA in the nursery.)

SCENE TWO

MARTHA. After another week of rain the high arch of blue sky appeared again and the sun which poured down was quite hot. Though there had been no chance to see Dickon, Mistress Mary had enjoyed herself very much, spending hours with Colin in his room. But on that first day when the sky was blue again, Mary could not wait to be outside. *(MUSIC OUT.)*

MARY. Isn't it a beautiful morning, Martha? Smell that good fresh air!

MARTHA. Aye, the air from th' moor has done thee good already. Even tha' hair doesn't slamp down on thy head so flat. *(She fluffs MARY's hair.)* Tha'rt not half so ugly when it's fluffed up a bit an' there's red in thy cheeks.

MARY. My hair is getting stronger just like me. Maybe if we can get Colin to go outside, he'll get stronger, too.

MARTHA. P'raps. He's not had a tantrum or a whining fit since tha's made friends with him. He wants to see thee right away.

MARY *(starting out the door).* I'll see him later. I'm going to be very busy in the garden.

MARTHA *(alarmed).* Eh! Miss Mary, it may put him all out of humor when I tell him that.

MARY. I can't stay. Dickon's waiting for me.

MARTHA. Oh, Miss Mary, please don't make me tell him.

MARY. Very well, I shall tell him myself.

MARTHA. Oh, Miss...

(MARY marches to COLIN's room, followed nervously by MARTHA.)

COLIN. Oh, there you are. Come and sit by me, but don't talk too loudly. My back aches and my head aches, I want you to sing to me again.

MARY *(remains standing).* I can't.

COLIN. Why not?

MARY. I have to go.

COLIN. Where?

MARY. Outside. Dickon is waiting for me.

COLIN. I won't let that boy come here if you go and stay with him instead of coming to talk with me.

MARY. If you send Dickon away, I'll never come to this room again.

COLIN. You'll have to if I want you.

MARY. I won't.

COLIN. I'll make you. They shall drag you in.

MARY. Shall they, Mr. Rajah? They may drag me in but they can't make me talk when they get me here. I'll sit and clench my teeth and never tell you one thing!

COLIN. You are a selfish beast!

MARY. What are you? Selfish people always say that. You're the most selfish boy I ever saw.

COLIN. I'm not as selfish as you, because I'm always ill, and I'm sure there is a lump coming on my back. And I'm going to die besides.

MARY. You're not!

COLIN. I am! You know I am! Everybody says so.

MARY. I don't believe it! You just say that to make people sorry. I believe you're proud of it. If you were a nice boy, it might be true—but you're too nasty!

COLIN. Get out of my room! Get out! Get out!! GET OUT! *(He throws a pillow at her. MARY catches the pillow and throws it back at him.)*

MARY. I will! And I'm not coming back! *(She starts out as COLIN begins to scream and cry hysterically. MARTHA looks on helplessly as MARY stops and turns back to COLIN. MARY stamps her foot.)* You stop it! *(She stamps again.)* I hate you! *(She stamps back into the room on the next lines until she is face to face with COLIN, topping his tantrum with her own.)* Everybody hates you! I wish everybody would run out of the house and let you scream yourself to death. You will scream yourself to death in a minute and I wish you would! *(COLIN pauses a moment, open-mouthed.)* If you scream another scream I'll scream too—and I can scream louder than you! *(She opens her mouth to scream.)*

COLIN. I can't stop! I can't!

MARY *(closes her mouth)*. You can. Mrs. Medlock says that half that ails you is hysterics and temper—just hysterics—*(She stamps her foot on each word.)* hysterics—*(Stamp.)* hysterics! *(Stamp.)*

COLIN. I felt the lump—I felt it.

MARY. You didn't feel a lump! If you did it was only a hysterical lump. There's nothing wrong with your horrid back. Turn over and let me look at it. Martha, come here and show me his back this minute!

MARTHA *(hesitates)*. What if he won't let me...

COLIN. Show her! Sh-she'll see then! *(MARTHA unbuttons the back of his nightshirt. MARY examines his back.)*

MARY. There's not a single lump there! Except backbone lumps and you can only feel them because you're so thin. There's not a lump as big as a pin! If you ever say there is again, I shall laugh!

MARTHA. I didn't know he thought he had a lump on his back. I could ha' told him there wasna' lump there.

COLIN *(calming down, but hiccupping a little.)* C-could you?

MARTHA. Yes, sir.

MARY. There!

COLIN. Do you think—I could—live to grow up?

MARTHA. I think so, sir, if you do what you are told to do and not give way to your temper and stay out a great deal in th' fresh air.

COLIN. I'll—I'll go out with you, Mary. I shan't hate fresh air if we can find the—*(MARY gives a warning cough. COLIN shuts up.)* I should like to go outside with you.

MARTHA. Tha' must try an' rest now, Mester Colin.

MARY. I will put him to sleep. You may go if you like, Martha.

MARTHA. Well, if he doesn't go to sleep in half an hour, tha' must call me.

MARY. I will. *(MARTHA leaves.)*

COLIN. I almost told, but I stopped myself in time. Do you—do you think you will find out anything at all about the way into the secret garden?

MARY. Yes. I think I already have in fact. And if you will go to sleep I will tell you tomorrow.

COLIN. Oh, Mary! If I could get into it I think I should live to grow up! Do you suppose—would you tell me softly as you did that first night—what you imagine it looks like inside? I am sure it will make me go to sleep.

MARY. Yes. Shut your eyes.

(COLIN shuts his eyes and MARY begins to describe the secret garden. As she does so the "garden theme" plays and lights slowly come up on DICKON as he begins to unfold more of the secret garden.)

MARY. I think it has been left alone so long—that it has grown all into a lovely tangle. I think the roses have climbed and climbed and climbed until they hang from the branches and walls and creep over the ground—almost like a strange, grey mist. Some of them have died but many—are alive *(MUSIC IN [III, #3].)* and when the summer comes there will be curtains and fountains of roses. Perhaps the leaves are beginning to break out and uncurl—and perhaps—the grey is changing and a green gauze veil is creeping over—everything. And the birds are coming to look at it—because it is—so safe and still. And perhaps—perhaps—perhaps—

(ROBIN enters and joins DICKON.)

MARY. The robin has found a mate—and is building a nest.

(MUSIC continues as COLIN falls asleep and MARY runs to join DICKON in the garden. ROBIN joins them, serenading. MUSIC continues under DICKON's lines.)

DICKON. Eh! Just listen to them birds—th' world seems full of 'em—all whistlin' an' pipin'. Look at 'em dartin' about an' hearken at 'em callin' to each other. Come springtime seems like as if all th' world's callin'.

MARY. Oh, Dickon, Dickon, I'm so happy, I can scarcely breathe! *(She whirls around in ecstasy. ROBIN chirps.)* Look, Dickon! *(Another chirp.)* It's the robin and he has something in his beak!

DICKON. Aye, we munnot stir. He'll stay here if we don't flight him. *(They carefully sit.)* He's settin' up housekeepin'. Us must keep still a bit an' try an' look as if us was grass an' trees an' bushes.

MARY. If we talk about him I can't help looking at him. We must talk of something else. There is something I must tell you.

DICKON. What is it?

MARY. Well—do you know about Colin?

DICKON. I've heard Martha speak of him.

MARY. I've seen him. I have been to talk to him every day. We argued, but we've made it up. He likes to hear me talk about the garden, he says it makes him forget about being ill and dying.

DICKON. If he was out here he wouldn't be thinkin' of dyin', he'd be watchin' for buds to break on bushes, an' likely he'd be healthier.

MARY. I've thought of that almost every time I've talked to him. I've wondered if he could keep a secret and I've wondered if we could bring him here without anyone seeing us. I have a plan, but I don't know if it will work.

DICKON. Eh! My! We mun get him out here—we mun get him watchin' an' listenin' an' sniffin' up th' air an' get him just soaked with sunshine. An' we munnot lose no time about it.

MARY *(carefully and proudly trying out her Yorkshire).* Aye, that we mun. I'll tell thee what us'll do first. He's took a graidely fancy to thee. When I go back to th' house to talk to him I'll ax him if tha' canna' come and see him an' bring thy creatures with thee...an' then—in a bit, we'll get him to come here an' show him everything.

DICKON *(amused).* Tha' mun talk a bit o' Yorkshire like that to Mester Colin. Tha'll make him laugh an' Mother says there's nowt as good for ill folks as laughin' is.

MARY. I'm going to talk Yorkshire to him this very day. *(MUSIC IN [III, #4]. MARY leaves and DICKON closes the door of the secret garden.)*

(Lights up on COLIN's room as MARY enters.)

COLIN. You smell like flowers and fresh things! What is it you smell of? It's cool and warm and sweet all at the same time!

MARY. It's th' wind from the moor. It comes o' sittin' on th' grass under a tree wi' Dickon an' his creatures. It's th' springtime as smells so graidely.

COLIN. What are you doing? I've never heard you talk like that before.

MARY. I'm givin' thee a bit o' Yorkshire.

COLIN. How funny it sounds!

MARY. Doesn't tha' understand a bit o' Yorkshire, an' tha' a Yorkshire lad thysel'?

COLIN. Do it some more!

MARY. Eh! I wonder tha'rt not ashamed o' thy face!

COLIN *(laughing in delight)*. That's wonderful!

MARY. It has come, Colin, the springtime has come. Dickon says so.

COLIN. Well, open the window. Perhaps we shall hear golden trumpets!

MARY *(goes to the window and throws it open)*. That's the fresh air you smell, now, Colin. Take long breaths of it, like Dickon does. He says it makes him feel as if he could live forever and ever!

COLIN. Forever and ever! Does it make him feel like that? *(And he takes some deep breaths.)* Mary...I'm sorry for saying what I did about sending Dickon away.

MARY. I'm glad.

COLIN. I should like to see him.

MARY. Really?

COLIN. Really.

MARY. Can I trust you? I trusted Dickon because birds trusted him. Can I trust you—for sure—for sure?

COLIN. Yes. Yes!

MARY. Well, Dickon will come to see you this afternoon, and he'll bring his creatures with him.

COLIN. Oh!

MARY. But that's not all. The rest is better. There is a door into the garden. It is under the ivy on the wall.

COLIN. Oh! Mary! Shall I see it? Shall I get into it? Shall I live to get into it?

MARY. Of course you'll live to get into it. Don't be silly.

COLIN. I dreamt about it all night long. I dreamt of the roses and the robin—just as you described it. It sounded just as if you'd seen it. *(There is a pause as MARY considers him.)*

MARY. I had seen it—and I had been in. I found the key and got in weeks ago. But I daren't tell you—I daren't because I was so afraid I couldn't trust you for sure!

COLIN *(gasps in delight)*. Tell me, Mary. Tell me all about it!

(Lights up on MRS. MEDLOCK as DR. CRAVEN enters.)

MRS. MEDLOCK. Oh, Doctor, I'm so glad you've come. The boy...

DR. CRAVEN. How is he? I heard he had another tantrum last night.. The boy will break a blood vessel in one of his fits someday.

MRS. MEDLOCK. Well, sir, you'll scarcely believe it. That plain, sourfaced child that's almost as bad as himself has bewitched him. How she's done it there's no telling. Come and look, sir, it's past crediting.

(MRS. MEDLOCK leads DR. CRAVEN to COLIN's room where he and MARY are deep in conversation.)

COLIN. Those long spires of blue ones—we'll have a lot of those. They're called Del-phin-i-ums...

MARY. Dickon says...*(She coughs as she sees DR. CRAVEN and MRS. MEDLOCK.)*

DR. CRAVEN. I'm sorry to hear you were ill last night, my boy.

COLIN. I'm better now—much better. I am going out in my chair in a day or two. I want some fresh air.

DR. CRAVEN. I thought you did not like fresh air.

COLIN. I don't when I am by myself but my cousin is going out with me. A very strong boy I know will push my carriage.

DR. CRAVEN. He must be a strong boy and a steady boy. And I must know something about him. Who is he?

MARY. It's Dickon.

DR. CRAVEN. Oh, Dickon.

MRS. MEDLOCK. If it is Dickon, he'll be safe enough.

DR. CRAVEN. Well, if it amuses you perhaps it won't do any harm. But you must remember...

COLIN. I don't want to remember. If there was a doctor anywhere who could make you forget you were ill instead of remembering it I would have him brought here.

DR. CRAVEN. Well, well, well...

COLIN. And Medlock...

MRS. MEDLOCK. Yes, sir?

COLIN. Dickon is going to visit me today. He is bringing a fox, a crow, two squirrels and a newborn lamb. You can tell Martha to bring them here.

MRS. MEDLOCK. I hope the aimals won't bite, sir.

COLIN. Dickon is an animal charmer. Charmer's animals never bite.

MARY. There are snake charmers in India that can put their snakes heads in their mouths.

MRS. MEDLOCK. Goodness!

COLIN. That is all. *(MRS. MEDLOCK and DR. CRAVEN leave, discussing COLIN when out of earshot.)*

MRS. MEDLOCK. Well, sir, could you have believed it?

DR. CRAVEN. It is certainly a new state of affairs. And there's no denying it is better than the old one. *(COLIN and MARY are heard laughing in delight as the lights fade and the scene changes. MUSIC IN [III, #5].)*

SCENE THREE

MARTHA. They were obliged to wait more than a week because first there came some very windy days and then Colin was threatened with a cold, which two things happening one after the other would no doubt have thrown him into a rage but that there was so much careful planning to do. The most absorbing thing, however, was the preparations to be made before Colin could be transported with sufficient secrecy to the garden.

(DICKON pushes COLIN onstage, accompanied by MARY, DR. CRAVEN and MRS. MEDLOCK.)

COLIN. Now, if the fresh air agrees with me, I may go out every day. Remember, none of the gardeners are to be anywhere near the long walk by the garden walls. No one is to be there. Everyone must keep away until I send word that they may go back to their work.

MRS. MEDLOCK. Very good, sir.

DR. CRAVEN. I'll call later, after you have come in. I must see how the going out agrees with you. I do wish you would let Mrs. Medlock or myself accompany you.

COLIN. Are you suggesting that my cousin and Dickon are not to be trusted? I don't like that suggestion.

DR. CRAVEN. No, no, I wasn't suggesting anything of the sort. We'll try this experiment.

COLIN. Very well...Mary, what is that thing you say in India when you have finished talking and want people to go?

MARY. You say, "You have my permission to go."

COLIN. Medlock, Doctor, you have my permission to go.

MRS. MEDLOCK and DR. CRAVEN. Yes, sir. *(They leave. MARY, COLIN and DICKON giggle.)*

COLIN. We're safe now. *(MUSIC [III, #6] accompanies MARY, DICKON and COLIN as DICKON pushes COLIN's chair along the garden walk.)* There are so many sounds of singing and humming and calling out...What is that scent the puffs of wind bring?

DICKON. It's the gorse on th' moor that's openin' out. Eh! Th' bees are at it wonderful today.

MARY. This is where the robin flew over the wall. And that is where he perched on the little heap of earth and showed me the key...And this is the ivy the wind pushed back...And here is the handle, and here is the door...*(She opens it slowly.)* Dickon, push him in, push him in quickly! *(MUSIC OUT. With a strong, sturdy push DICKON does so as MARY opens the door and the garden is revealed.)*

COLIN. It's beautiful! Mary! Dickon! I shall get well! I shall get well! And I shall live forever and ever! *(MUSIC [III, #7] underscores the narration as COLIN, MARY and DICKON make the garden grow.)*

(BEN enters from another side of the stage.)

BEN. One of the strange things about living in the world is that it is only now and then that one is quite sure one is going to live forever and ever. One knows it sometimes when one gets up at the tender, solemn dawn time and goes out and stands alone and throws one's head far back and looks up and up and watches the pale sky slowly changing and flushing and marvelous things happening until the east almost makes one cry out and one's heart stands still at the strange unchanging maj-

Act III   THE SECRET GARDEN   Page 67

esty of the sun...Then sometimes the immense quiet of the dark blue at night with millions of stars waiting and watching makes one sure; and sometimes a sound of far-off music makes it true; and sometimes a look in someone's eyes...*(Exits as DICKON speaks.)*

DICKON. Seems to me like I never see'd an afternoon as graidely as this 'ere.

MARY. I'll warrant it's the graidliest one as ever was in this world.

COLIN. Does tha' think as happen it was made loike this 'ere all o' purpose for me?

DICKON. My word! That there is a bit o' good Yorkshire. Tha'rt shapin' first-rate, that tha'rt.

COLIN *(noticing his mother's tree)*. That's a very old tree over there, isn't it?

DICKON *(exchanging a look with MARY)*. Yes.

COLIN. It looks as if a big branch had been broken off. I wonder how it was done.

DICKON. It's been done many a year.

(ROBIN appears and softly lands on the old tree.)

DICKON. Eh! Look at that robin! *(COLIN wheels away to look at ROBIN. DICKON takes MARY aside.)* We could never tell him how the tree was broken, poor lad. If he says anything about it we mun try to look cheerful.

MARY. Aye, that we mun.

DICKON. Mrs. Craven was a very lovely young lady. An' Mother says she thinks she's about Misselthwaite still, lookin' after Mester Colin, same as all mothers do.

COLIN *(turning back to them)*. I don't want this afternoon to go. But I'm going to come back here every day. I'm going to see everything grow. I'm going to grow here myself. *(MUSIC fades.)*

DICKON. That tha' will. Us'll have thee walkin' about here an' diggin' same as other folk afore long.

COLIN. Walk! Dig! Shall I?

DICKON. For sure tha' will. Tha's got legs o' thine own, same as other folks.

MARY *(warningly)*. Dickon...

COLIN *(unperturbed)*. Nothing really ails them, but they are so thin and weak. I'm afraid to try and stand on them.

DICKON. When tha' stops bein' afraid tha'll stand on 'em.

(COLIN looks up and sees BEN peering at them from over the wall. BEN is speechless with anger.)

COLIN. Who is that man?

BEN *(to MARY)*. If I wasn't a bachelder an' tha' was a wench o' mine, I'd give thee a hidin'. I never knowed how tha' got so thick wi' me. If it hadna' been for the robin...

MARY. Ben Weatherstaff, it was the robin who showed me the way.

BEN. Tha' bad young'un, layin' thy badness on a robin. *(Unable to contain his curiosity.)* Eh! Tha' young nowt—however in th' world did tha' get in!?

MARY. I can't tell you from here while you're shakin' your fist at me.

COLIN. Dickon, wheel me over there! *(DICKON does so.)* Do you know who I am? Answer me!

BEN *(staring in amazement)*. Aye, that I do—wi' thy mother's eyes starin' at me out o' tha' face. Tha'rt th' poor cripple.

COLIN. I'm not a cripple.

MARY. He's not! He's not got a lump as big as a pin!

BEN. Tha' hasn't got a crooked back?

COLIN. No!

BEN. Tha' hasn't got crooked legs?

COLIN and MARY. NO!

COLIN. Dickon! Come here! Come here this minute! *(MUSIC IN [III, #8]. DICKON runs to COLIN. MARY begins to gabble in excitement as she realizes what COLIN means to do.)*

MARY. He can do it he can do it he can do it he can he can!

COLIN *(leaning on DICKON's shoulders, he stands)*. Look at me—you! Just look!

DICKON. He's as straight as I am! He's as straight as any lad in Yorkshire!

BEN. Eh! Th' lies folks tells. There's not a knob on thee. Tha'lt make a mon yet. God bless thee!

COLIN. Get down from that ladder and come in here. We did not want you, but now you will have to be in the secret. Be quick!

BEN *(scrambling down from the ladder)*. Eh! Lad. Eh! My lad! Yes, sir! Yes, sir!

COLIN *(to MARY)*. Go and meet him.

MARY *(goes, still muttering to herself)*. You can do it! You can do it! I told you you could! You can do it. You can! *(She is out.)*

COLIN *(to DICKON)*. I can stand.

DICKON. I told thee tha' could as soon as tha's stopped bein' afraid.

COLIN *(suspiciously)*. Are you making magic?

DICKON. Tha's doin' magic thysel'. It's same magic as made these 'ere work out o' th' earth.

COLIN. Aye, there couldna' be bigger magic than that there...I'm going to walk to that tree. Bring the rug from the chair.

(BEN enters.)

COLIN *(to BEN)*. Look at me! Am I a hunchback?

BEN. Nowt o' th' sort! But what did tha' shut thysel' up for?

COLIN. Everyone thought I was going to die. I'm not!

BEN. Tha' die! Tha's got too much pluck in thee. Sit thee down on th' rug, young Mester, an' give me my orders.

COLIN. What work do you do in the gardens, Weatherstaff?

BEN. Anythin' I'm told to. I'm kep' on by favor because tha' mother liked me.

COLIN. My mother? This was her garden, wasn't it?

BEN. Aye, it was that. She were main fond of it.

COLIN. I am fond of it, too. I am going to work here every day. I shall send for you to help sometimes...but only when no one can see you.

BEN. I've come here before when no one saw me.

MARY. But there was no door!

BEN. I come over th' wall. But th' rheumatics held me back th' last two year.

DICKON. Th' come an' did a bit o' prunin'!

BEN. "Ben," she said to me once, "if ever I go away, you must take care of my roses." When she did go away th' orders was no one was ever to come nigh. But I come. She'd gave her orders first.

COLIN. I'm glad you did it, Weatherstaff. You'll know how to keep a secret.

BEN. I'll know, sir. An' it'll be easier for a man wi' rheumatics to come in at th' door. *(COLIN has been absently digging in the earth. He picks up the trowel and looks at it.)*

COLIN *(to DICKON)*. Tha' said tha'd have me walkin' about an' diggin'—I thought tha' was just leein' to please me. This is th' first day an' I've walked—an' here I am diggin'.

BEN. How'd tha' like to plant a bit o' somethin'? I can get thee a rose in a pot.

COLIN. Go and get it! Quick! Quick! *(BEN leaves.)* Mary, Dickon, help me deepen the hole. *(MARY, DICKON and COLIN dig.)* I want to do it before the sun goes quite—quite down.

(BEN enters.)

BEN. Here, lad. Set it in th' earth thysel' same as a king does when he goes to a new place. *(MUSIC IN [III, #9]. ROBIN sings as BEN helps them plant the rose. As the music softens, the dialogue resumes, underscored.)*

DICKON. It's planted!

MARY. And the sun is only slipping over the edge.

COLIN. Help me up, Dickon. I want to be standing when it goes. That's part of the magic.

(Lights come down on the garden and come up on MRS. MEDLOCK and DR. CRAVEN in the house as MUSIC fades.)

DR. CRAVEN. He stays out in the garden a great deal. Where do you think he goes?

MRS. MEDLOCK. Lord knows. He won't let anyone follow him, excepting Miss Mary and Dickon.

DR. CRAVEN. His appetite is still good?

MRS. MEDLOCK. Enormous. Him an' Miss Mary both. But it's very strange...

DR. CRAVEN. What?

MRS. MEDLOCK. Well, when I complimented him on it, he suggested it was...unnatural. It's almost as if he didn't want anyone thinking he was well.

DR. CRAVEN. Yes. And when I mentioned writing to his father, he grew quite irritated.

SCENE FOUR

SCENE: *MUSIC [III, #10]. Lights up on BEN.*

BEN. While the secret garden was coming alive and two children were coming alive with it, there was a man wandering around certain faraway places in the Norwegian fjords and mountains of Switzerland, and he was a man who for ten years had kept his mind filled with dark and heartbroken thinking.

(MR. CRAVEN enters.)

BEN. He was a tall man with a drawn face and crooked shoulders and the name he always entered on hotel registers was...*(MUSIC OUT.)*

Act III   THE SECRET GARDEN   Page 73

MR. CRAVEN. Archibald Craven, Misselthwaite Manor, Yorkshire, England...I've come so far, yet I can't escape...The valley is so still...except this little stream, which almost seems alive...And the light...I never noticed—touching the mountains—it looks as if the world is just being born. What is happening? I almost feel...I don't understand...I almost feel as if *I* were alive!

(MUSIC IN [III, #11]. Lights up on COLIN's room. MARY, COLIN and DICKON are joyfully stuffing their mouths with currant buns. MARTHA's voice is heard.)

MARTHA *(off)*. Art tha' in, Mester Colin? I have thy tea! *(With much giggling, MARY and DICKON get COLIN into bed. COLIN makes an attempt at sounding weak, as they ALL hurriedly try to finish eating the last of their food.)*
COLIN. Come in...

(MARTHA enters.)

MARTHA. Here, Mester Colin. See what wonderful things Cook's sent up to thee.
COLIN. I don't want it.
MARTHA. Not want it? But tha's eaten nothing in two days. And tha' was doin' so well before.
COLIN. I told you it was an unnatural appetite. *(MARY starts to laugh and tries to stifle it, almost choking in the process.)*
MARTHA. What's the matter?
MARY. It was something between a sneeze and a cough and it got into my throat.

MARTHA *(looks at DICKON who only shrugs).* Well, I'm fair mothered to death wi' th' both of ye! And Dickon, tha'rt just as bad! *(She slams the tray down and stalks out.)*

MARY. Martha, we didn't mean...

DICKON. I'll make it right with her.

COLIN. Please do, Dickon. I don't want Martha to be angry. *(DICKON goes outside the room and approaches MARTHA.)*

DICKON. 'Ere, Martha, us weren't laughin' at you.

MARTHA. Eh! I know that, Dickon. But there's somethin' mysterious happenin' in this house an' I'm worried about Mester Colin.

DICKON. Don't tha' be worryin' about him. He's as healthy as a young hawk.

MARTHA. Then why won't he eat?

DICKON. Martha, I've got a secret to keep. It's not a bad 'un, tha' knows that.

MARTHA. Is it about Mester Colin?

DICKON. Aye, but it's no worse than hidin' where a bird's nest is. Tha' doesn't mind it, does tha'?

MARTHA. If tha'rt in it, then it must be a good secret.

DICKON. There's a good girl!

MARTHA. An' Mester Colin is really gettin' better?

DICKON. He's so better that when his father comes home he won't be recognizin' him.

MARTHA. Eh! Mester Craven mun come home soon!

DICKON. Aye. Th' lad doesn't say so, but he misses him, I can tell.

MARTHA. Then someone mun send word to him. An' I know just th' person!

DICKON. Who?

MARTHA. If tha' can have thy secrets, I can have mine. *(MUSIC, lights up on house. MARTHA exits.)*

(Lights up on COLIN and MARY as DICKON shrugs. He pops into the room, gives a thumbs-up sign and leaves. COLIN and MARY shout for joy.)

COLIN. Hooray!

MARY. Shhh!

COLIN *(sighs)*. I wish my father would come home. I can't go on pretending like this much longer. Now that I am a real boy my legs and body are so full of magic that I can't keep them still...I wish it wasn't raining today. *(MUSIC IN [III, #12].)*

MARY. Colin, do you know how many rooms there are in this house?

COLIN. About a thousand, I suppose.

MARY. There's about a hundred, all locked up.

COLIN. It sounds like a secret garden. Suppose we go and look at them. You could wheel me in my chair when we got into the hall.

MARY. That's what I was thinking. *(They start out. MARY notices Mrs. Craven's picture.)* Colin...

COLIN. I know what you want me to tell you...I'm going to keep the curtain drawn back.

MARY. Why?

COLIN. Because it doesn't make me angry anymore to see her. I want to see her laughing all the time. I think she must have been a magic sort of person, perhaps.

MARY. You are so like her now that sometimes I think you are her ghost made into a boy.

COLIN. If I were her ghost—my father would be fond of me.

(They exit as lights come up on MR. CRAVEN. MARTHA enters above MR. CRAVEN. MUSIC changes.)

MARTHA. As the golden summer changed into the deep golden autumn, Mr. Craven went to the Lake of Como. There he found the loveliness of a dream. And it was there that a certain letter found its way to him. *(MR. CRAVEN takes a letter from his vest pocket and begins to read it aloud.)*

MR. CRAVEN. "Dear Sir, I am Susan Sowerby that made bold to speak to you once on the moor..." Susan Sowerby? Ah, yes. Martha and Dickon's mother...It was about Miss Mary I spoke...*(MUSIC OUT.)* That's right. Miss Mary and her bit of earth...*(Reads again.)* "Please, sir, I would come home if I were you..." Home...Perhaps I should. But, Colin...No, I don't think I could bear to look at Colin just yet.

(MR. CRAVEN freezes as lights come up on COLIN, MARY, DICKON and BEN in the garden.)

COLIN. Mary! Dickon! Just look at me. I'm well!

MARY. Aye, that tha'rt.

COLIN. I feel as if I want to shout out something—something thankful, joyful! Something magic!

BEN *(gruffly)*. Tha' might sing th' Doxology.

COLIN. What is that?

BEN. Dickon can sing it for thee, I'll warrant.

DICKON. They sing it in church. Mother says she believes th' skylarks sing it when they get up in th' mornin'.

COLIN. Then it must be a nice song. Sing it, Dickon. I want to hear it.

Act III THE SECRET GARDEN Page 77

DICKON. Tha' must take off tha' cap, an' so mun tha', Ben, an' tha' mun stand up, tha' knows...(*As they prepare to sing, MR. CRAVEN sits. He continues to read the letter.*)

MR. CRAVEN. "Please sir, I would come home if I was you. I think you would be glad to come and if you will excuse me, sir—I think your lady would ask you to come if she was here. Your obedient servant, Susan Sowerby." My lady...Lilias...Ten years...(*His head nods as he begins to fall asleep.*) Too late...too late...

DICKON (*using his pipe to get a note, he begins to sing, his voice floating angelically. MUSIC [III, #13]*). Praise God from whom all blessings flow...(*A WOMAN's voice is heard softly calling above the music.*)

WOMAN'S VOICE. Archie...Archie...

MR. CRAVEN (*lifting his head*). Lilias? Lilias, where are you?

DICKON. Praise him all creatures here below...

WOMAN'S VOICE. In the garden...

MR. CRAVEN. In the garden? But the door is locked and the key is buried deep.

DICKON. Praise him above ye heavenly host...

WOMAN'S VOICE. In the garden, Archie...

DICKON. Praise father, son and holy ghost...(*MR. CRAVEN wakes up on the word "ghost," looks at the letter in his hand, folds it.*)

MR. CRAVEN. I will go back to Misselthwaite. I'll go at once.

(*The lights fade on MR. CRAVEN as he exits to return home and come up full on MARY, COLIN and DICKON in the secret garden as they continue their celebration. The door is shut on the garden as MR.*

CRAVEN re-enters. MUSIC underscores to the end of the play.)

MR. CRAVEN. I will try to find the key. I will try to open the door. I must—though I don't know why.

(MRS. MEDLOCK enters.)

MRS. MEDLOCK. Mr. Craven! We did not expect...
MR. CRAVEN. How is Master Colin, Medlock?
MRS. MEDLOCK. Master Colin, sir? Well, sir, he's different in a manner of speaking.
MR. CRAVEN. Worse?
MRS. MEDLOCK. To tell the truth, sir, Master Colin might be better and he might be changing for the worse. His appetite, sir, is past understanding and his ways...
MR. CRAVEN. Where is Master Colin now?
MRS. MEDLOCK. He's in the garden, sir. He's always...
MR. CRAVEN. In the garden!

(MR. CRAVEN leaves MRS. MEDLOCK and enters the garden path. As he approaches the door of the secret garden he almost collides with COLIN who is triumphantly finishing a race with DICKON and MARY close behind.)

MR. CRAVEN. What—Who—
COLIN *(breathlessly)*. Father!! I'm Colin. You can't believe it. I scarcely can believe it myself. I'm Colin!
MR. CRAVEN *(connecting his dream and reality in joyous discovery)*. In the garden...

COLIN. Yes. It was the garden that did it—and Mary and Dickon and the creatures. Aren't you glad, Father? Aren't you glad? I'm going to live forever and ever!

(They exit as MUSIC fades and lights come up on MRS. MEDLOCK and BEN.)

MRS. MEDLOCK. Did you see either of them, Weatherstaff?
BEN. Aye, that I did.
MRS. MEDLOCK. Both of them?
BEN. Both of 'em.
MRS. MEDLOCK. Together?
BEN. Together, ma'am.
MRS. MEDLOCK. Where was Master Colin? How did he look? What did they say to each other?
BEN. I didna' hear that, along o' only bein' on th' stepladder lookin' over the wall. But I'll tell thee this... *(MUSIC resumes.)*...there's things goin' on outside as you house people knows nowt about. An' what tha'll find out tha'll find out soon...Look there if tha's curious. Look what's comin' across the grass.

(MUSIC swells triumphantly as the door of the secret garden is flung open by MARY and DICKON. COLIN and MR. CRAVEN walk through. MARTHA and DR. CRAVEN enter from opposite sides.)

MARTHA. Across the lawn came the master of Misselthwaite.
DR. CRAVEN. And he looked as many of them had never seen him.

MRS. MEDLOCK. And by his side with his head up in the air...

BEN. And his eyes full of laughter...

DICKON. Walked as strongly and steadily as any boy in Yorkshire...

MARY. Master Colin! *(MUSIC swells as COLIN and MR. CRAVEN, flanked by MARY and DICKON, walk to center and the lights fade.)*

CURTAIN—END OF PLAY

ABOUT THE AUTHOR OF THE BOOK

Frances Hodgson Burnett was born November 24, 1849 in Manchester, England. During Frances' teen years, her family fell into hard times and emigrated to America to live in rural Tennessee. Frances lived there until her marriage in 1873.

In 1886, Burnett wrote *Little Lord Fauntleroy* which brought her fame, wealth, and respect among literary circles. The story later became a successful play and movie in 1914 starring Mary Pickford. Burnett wrote *Sara Crewe* in 1888 as a rags to riches story, and later revised and republished it under the title *A Little Princess* in 1905. In the 1930s, *A Little Princess* was made into a popular film starring Shirley Temple.

In 1898, Burnett returned to England. She was desperately unhappy over the death of her older son and began gardening to seek solace from her pain. Burnett was freed from her sorrow out of her love for growing things and out of that experience came the inspiration for the story of *The Secret Garden*.

Having touched the edges of a profound truth, Frances Hodgson Burnett created the story of a girl and boy whose natures have been badly warped but who recover through the discovery that selflessness opens a secret door to happiness.

PLAYWRIGHT'S NOTES

"Just tell the story..." Excellent advice for an actor and a director, but most importantly for a playwright and particularly for a playwright who adapts another's story to the stage. But as usual, the simplest advice is not always the easiest to follow. Not all stories travel easily to the stage and there are always inherent difficulties in translating from one medium to another. Therefore, I approached adapting *THE SECRET GARDEN* by Frances Hodgson Burnett with a garden variety of emotions—a great deal of love and excitement mixed with some fear and trepidation. *THE SECRET GARDEN* is not only one of my favorite books, but it is also a classic beloved by many generations of readers since its first publication in 1911. That meant that there were a lot of people besides myself who felt they personally knew the characters and who would not be happy if they were mistreated. I was excited by the opportunity to share this lovely story with a new production. But there is a heavy responsibility in making a favorable first impression, as well as doing justice to the original. There were obvious technical difficulties to consider as well; a garden which grows on stage, several animal characters including a very important robin, a forbidding English manor house, and the awesome Yorkshire moors in all their mystery and beauty. But at the center of *THE SECRET GARDEN* is drama; a suspenseful story, fascinating characters and beautiful dialogue. I decided to concentrate on these and let the magic of theatre take care of the "special effects."

And finally I remembered another piece of advice often given to theatre artists..."Trust your material." Adapting *THE SECRET GARDEN* has been a lesson in trust for me. In trusting the material I have also come to trust my own love and care for the story. I've tried to craft it well and carefully for the stage. I trust that you will enjoy it, and that Frances Hodgson Burnett would approve.

COMPOSER'S NOTES

I read *THE SECRET GARDEN* for the first time last year. Yes, believe it or not, I missed it while I was growing up. But for some strange reason, I felt a twinge of familiarity as I dashed through the pages on a Saturday train ride to Chicago. With Burnett's beautiful melodic prose I rediscovered the small and significant triumph of growing up, with all the strength and clear-eyed vision it produces. I felt the warmth of true friendship and the joy of dashing breathless through the morning grass. I also felt the aloneness that childhood sometimes brings.

THE SECRET GARDEN is a melody of words that sing of the magical, unpredictable turns that life sometimes offers. Along with Mary and Colin, I discovered parts of myself I had left behind longer ago than I care to imagine.

So, as I read, I listened to the story and to the music in my head. The book became like a film and I began to hear the soundtrack. The music you will hear is exactly what I heard as I read Burnett's beautiful book. In a way it is her music, not mine, influenced by the color, cadence, and clarity of her writing.

Each major character is represented by a musical theme. So is the Garden itself. The robin's voice is the flute. The music was inspired by the book, but also by a clever little robin that chirped outside in my backyard all summer. He kept saying, "Listen to me! Listen to me!!", so I did, and to him I am most grateful.

The music is often used in a traditional musical theatre sense, to help with scene changes and to begin and end the piece in a consistent style. Music is often utilized to underscore the spoken word and to add texture and emotional color. It is my hope that the music does what a good illustration should do: add an extra dimension to the experience of the story. When you read, you reach into a book. In the theatre, the story should reach out to you, and that's why the music is there. To reach out. Pam Sterling's faithful adaptation, the music, and of course Burnett's wonderful tale have been carefully mixed to allow a simple, profound story to fill an empty stage. We have added a few voices. The story will speak for itself.

The music for *THE SECRET GARDEN* is dedicated to my friend, Pam Sterling.

ABOUT STORY THEATRE

In this script of *THE SECRET GARDEN*, the playwright has used a dramatic technique called story theatre. In traditional plays, the audience is shown a character's feelings through action or through a character's behavior (what the character says or does). The environment in a traditional play is created primarily through sets and costumes. Story theatre borrows from storytelling techniques in that it asks the audience to use their imaginations to see environment as a narrator describes it and also allows for the play to progress smoothly from scene to scene instead of stopping to change sets in a blackout. This technique of story theatre works well for stage adaptations of books, particularly classics, because it may utilize the familiar words of the author to describe a scene which would be difficult to create onstage. Many new plays have used this technique, for instance, adaptations of Charles Dickens' novels *Great Expectations* and *Nicholas Nickleby*, as well as the current Broadway hit *Les Misérables*, which is adapted from the novel by Victor Hugo.

DIRECTOR'S NOTES

DIRECTOR'S NOTES

DIRECTOR'S NOTES

DIRECTOR'S NOTES